AMERICAN MUSIC

American

THE CHICAGO HISTORY OF AMERICAN CIVILIZATION

Daniel J. Boorstin, EDITOR

Music

Irving Sablosky

THE UNIVERSITY OF CHICAGO PRESS

CHICAGO AND LONDON

International Standard Book Number: 0–226–73324–6

Library of Congress Catalog Card Number: 79–78094

THE UNIVERSITY OF CHICAGO PRESS, CHICAGO 60637
THE UNIVERSITY OF CHICAGO PRESS, LTD., LONDON

to My Father

I resist any thing better than my own diversity.
Whitman, *Song of Myself*

Editor's Preface

Wherever we go in the world today we hear American music. Where English is not spoken or read, where American history and ways of life are unknown, where the facts of the contemporary United States are perverted or prohibited, the strains of American music can be heard. Our music is not only the most far-reaching, but also the most eloquent spokesman of our civilization.

In this book, Mr. Sablosky helps us hear what it can tell us about America. What, he asks, has been peculiarly American about the music composed and performed in the United States? Musical forms elsewhere separated for aristocratic and for popular audiences here have been combined: opera and folksong merge into musical comedy. Regional and national strains which elsewhere run in separate streams here produce new mixtures: African, West Indian voodoo, Spanish, Caribbean, and French

Editor's Preface

folksongs merge into a wonderful New Orleans jazz. Song and dance have never been more intimately or more indiscriminately married. In America, if anywhere, we see the illusoriness of "pure" forms. The story of American music which our author tells is a vividly American story. Old World forms and Old World peoples produce—sometimes collaboratively, sometimes anonymously, and often spontaneously—surprising new formulas which become a motley extravaganza of New World music.

Just as the jostling and mixing of peoples have produced new varieties of music, so American technology and American wealth have produced vast new audiences. The phonograph, then radio, and then television, brought grand opera companies, symphony orchestras, and string ensembles into the living rooms and kitchens of the populace, at the same time they brought popular music to the ears of musical snobs. For the first time in history a whole nation—young and old, rich and poor, urban and rural, crude and cultivated—became a musical audience.

While the older musical forms reached more people than ever before, newer forms were produced for the new audiences. Then, as Mr. Sablosky explains, these audiences themselves helped shape our music.

To tell this grand, complex story in a brief volume, to talk about the sounds of music without being either technical or pedantic, is as difficult a task as has faced any of the authors in our series. But Mr. Sablosky has done the job for us, and all along the way he has enlivened his learning with a contagious enthusiasm. I cannot imagine anyone so tone-deaf that he will not be persuaded that our music deserves a more prominent place in the story of American civilization. Our music has too often been treated as "background" for momentous events. Mr.

Editor's Preface

Sablosky brings it into the foreground where we hear the leit-motifs of all American civilization.

In doing this he has admirably served the purpose of the "Chicago History of American Civilization," which aims to make every aspect of our past a window to all our history. The series contains two kinds of books: a *chronological* group, which provides a coherent narrative of American history from the beginning to the present day, and a *topical* group, which deals with the history of varied and significant aspects of American life. This book is one of the topical group.

DANIEL J. BOORSTIN

Table of Contents

Contents

Part One

NEW BEGINNINGS

I

First Encounters

One tries in vain to see the development of American music or any single phase of it as a simple organic process of growth. Rather, it developed, like the country itself, from a number of different starting points and in a number of different directions at once. It was always the product of at least two different forces, and usually of more, meeting like vectors in a mathematician's diagram, each encounter working irretrievable changes in the quality, quantity, and direction of the forces coming together.

The first such meeting for American music was that of the musical practice of seventeenth-century Englishmen with the continent of North America. St. John Crèvecoeur has vividly described the changes wrought in the character of the settlers by their encounter with the land they were to make their home: as they sought to create of the land a new England, it created of them the new American. They changed not through some charm or magic exerted upon them by the New World; they changed of necessity. So too did their music.

The first colonists left behind them an England just past her Elizabethan musical peak. The church music of Thomas Tallis, William Byrd, and Orlando Gibbons, the songs and lute music of John Dowland, the keyboard music of John Bull, the airs and madrigals of Thomas Morley and others brought England to a musical eminence she was scarcely to know again. Only a decade before the London Company planted its Virginia settlement at Jamestown, Morley published his *Plaine and Easie Introduction to Practicall Musicke* to help the conscientious English gentleman sing his part properly in a madrigal—the assumption being that a true gentleman could or would want to.

Few of Virginia's early settlers were born gentlemen. Shipping people, sons of merchants, squires, or yeomen were the highest among them, and men who arrived as servants later became burgesses. Still, if life in America could change English townsfolk into rough frontiersmen, it could also change English tradesmen and even bondsmen into plantation owners. As early Virginians began to acquire land and from the land gained wealth, they also began to hanker after the ways of England's landed gentry. Even before the seventeenth century was out, ships that came up the waterways to the thriving tobacco plantations brought lutes, virginals, violins, oboes, and flageolets for the planters' pleasure.

The transplanting of English music at fullest flower to a scattering of plantations in America was nevertheless a patent impossibility. No doubt music—whether madrigals or psalms—afforded the lonely planters, their families, and their servants grateful relief from the monotony of life in so remote a place.

4

First Encounters

No doubt they sang, too, familiar songs and ballads, inventing new verses (or whole new versions) reflecting their American experience. And as Negro servants or slaves became part of the plantation scene they were quickly encouraged to learn to fiddle jigs and reels for dancing. But even 170 years after the founding of the Jamestown colony, one of the new planter aristocracy to whom music was most dear, Thomas Jefferson, lamented in a letter the "state of deplorable barbarism" in which music found itself in Virginia.

For music, as for the people who came to America, there would have to be a new beginning in the new land. It would not be made in Virginia from the heights of Tudor church music or the instrumental music of fashionable England, but from simple psalmody and the homely musical practice of families settling a New England wilderness.

For the Pilgrims and the Puritans, the achievements of Byrd, Morley, and the rest were exactly the sort of frivolity and "popery" from which the voyages of the *Mayflower*, the *Arabella*, and the ships of the great migration of the 1630's promised blessed deliverance. Out of their zeal for reform came a new American institution, the New England singing school. It was the first embodiment of an approach which was to make its influence felt in American music from that time on.

Like so much of Puritan invention, the singing school grew out of controversy. The story of its growth begins almost with the landing of the Pilgrims and extends over a century's time.

New England's founders were not so grimly set against all music as fading legend would have them. For these ardent believers, music like good beer and wine was a gift of the Creator, to be sanctified through use in His praise. The danger was that it could become a corrupting influence, a distraction from godly thoughts. Its proper use was in the singing of the psalms, and this was encouraged in the meeting house and in the home, so that every impulse to song would at the same time be an impulse to worship.

The Pilgrims brought with them to Plymouth a psalter prepared especially for them by the theologian Henry Ainsworth during their sojourn in Leyden. In it, newly versified psalm texts were set to thirty-nine tunes selected from the old Sternhold and Hopkins psalm book of 1562, then the most widely used English version of the psalms. Ainsworth had purified those verses in which Sternhold and Hopkins's poetic license had drawn the Separatists' disapproval. Evidently the Puritans of Massachusetts Bay shared their reservations: "Gods Altar needs not our polishings," explained Richard Mather, and he joined two other leading Massachusetts Bay ministers, John Eliot and Thomas Weld, in preparing for the faithful a new book of the psalms in English verse as plain and as close in literal meaning to the scriptural text as they could make it. It is significant that *The Whole Booke of Psalmes Faithfully Translated into English Metre* (Cambridge, Massachusetts, 1640) was the first book printed in New England, and probably the first in English on the North American continent.

The *Bay Psalm Book*, to call it by its familiar name, contained no music, but the Puritans knew the tunes to which its verses could be sung. The authors took care to make their versification faithful both to the meaning of the original Hebrew and to the meter of familiar psalm melodies. They reduced their verses to six metrical types, corresponding to the metrical patterns of tunes well known to churchgoers of the time. The first verse type alone, the reader was advised, would lend itself to singing "in very neere fourty common tunes." When a second edition of the *Bay Psalm Book* was printed in 1647, one of the colony's foremost ministers, John Cotton, sought to further the practice of singing from it. In a tract on *Singing of Psalmes a Gospel-Ordinance*, Cotton set it forth "for a Doctrine of Truth"

That singing of Psalms with a lively voice is an holy Duty of God's worship now in the dayes of the New Testament. When we say, singing with a lively voice, we suppose none will so farre misconstrue us as to think we exclude singing with the heart; for God is a Spirit: and to worship him with the voice without the spirit were but lip-labour. . . . But this we say. As we are to make melody in our hearts, so in our voices also.

Of the editions of the *Bay Psalm Book* that have survived, the ninth (1698) is the earliest that contains printed music: thirteen melodies to which the psalms could be sung, with instructions for matching psalm to tune. The decision to print the tunes suggests the elders' concern that the psalms should continue to be properly sung in a rapidly growing and changing community. The first Massachusetts Bay generation was sufficiently familiar with the melodies that they needed no printed guide. But as the tunes were passed from father and mother to sons and daughters, they were bound to change subtly, and doubts were bound to arise about what version of a given melody was correct. The need for a musical text was felt, and the addition of printed music to the *Bay Psalm Book* answered it.

But if printing the tunes was a measure taken in the hope of saving psalmody from the effects of change in the community, the American situation frustrated this hope. When their flock numbered only the thousand who came to Massachusetts Bay in 1630, the elders may have been able to hold congregational singing within whatever bounds they considered fit. Ten years later, New Englanders numbered nearly twenty thousand; nor were

7

they any longer within easy reach of the elders' persuasion. The leaders could strive to keep the church pure by expelling Roger Williams or Anne Hutchinson, but such dissidents needed only to move out of range of orthodox authority to continue their unorthodox practices.

A small congregation of literate folk like the earliest colonists in Massachusetts Bay could easily read the psalms from the *Bay Psalm Book* and sing them to tunes made familiar by long use; but as the great migration brought many less literate people to the colonies, the ability so to read and sing declined beyond the capacity of printed notes to save it. As the Halfway Covenant of 1662 sought (by automatically extending church membership to grandchildren of the "saints") to infuse new life into an orthodoxy menaced by changing circumstances, the practice of "lining out" or "deaconing" was introduced in the hope of keeping vital and meaningful the singing of the psalms. According to the new practice, the congregation would no longer sing a psalm through from start to finish. Instead, each line was sung, chanted or read out by a deacon, then sung in response by the assembly, which now included many who had neither a book nor the ability to read one. "Lining out," common then in England, had been disdained by the New England Puritans; now they came to it of necessity.

The solution created its own problems. Though lining out assured the meeting's unified progress through the verses of a psalm, it also slowed the proceedings down by a good half. A tune that might once have been sung "with a lively voice" was now dismembered and chanted slowly line by line. It was also misremembered, so that many a churchgoer became his own composer, singing the melody as he thought it ought to be. The contribution of New England individualism to this endeavor ought not to be underestimated.

First Encounters

It is also far from improbable that at the frontier, remote from any learned minister's hearing, many found the verses of the metrical psalms providentially adaptable to tunes of their favorite secular ballads. Eight of the thirteen tunes printed in the 1698 *Bay Psalm Book* were in "common meter"—in other words, ballad meter—and the psalms that had been versified to fit those tunes would neatly accommodate themselves to the tunes of any number of popular ballads. How early the American back-country settlers actually ventured to fit sacred texts to secular tunes we have no way of knowing; no doubt it was common practice before the end of the eighteenth century.

As the eighteenth century began, the musical result of Puritan psalmody's encounter with the conditions of American life was that psalm-singing declined to the point of chaos. It was the effort to bring it back to a state of order in the increasingly mobile and secular world of New England that led to the establishment of singing schools.

SINGING SCHOOLS: "THE PROGRESS OF IMPROVEMENT"

In music, as in all aspects of New England life, the orthodox leaders sought in vain to preserve their ancestral vision of Zion in the wilderness from the multiplying outside forces that eroded it. It was characteristic of them to look to schools as a practical solution. The decline of psalmody had come of ignorance; too many in the congregation simply did not know the proper tunes for the psalms. If people could be taught to sing the tunes correctly, as they were written in the psalter, the singing in meetings could be restored to order. In this spirit of reform, then, the first schools of singing were established in the second decade of the new century.

At this time, the Treaty of Utrecht (1713) secured Britain's supremacy on the seas and inaugurated a period of peace that spanned a generation. This, plus discontent in rural Ireland and Scotland, brought a new surge of immigration to render the New England ministers' authority more tenuous than ever. The newly instituted singing schools met no easy success. Too few of the settlers knew anything of musical notation, and not many were interested in acquiring the knowledge.

Two young Harvard divines published books in an effort to solve the problem. They were Thomas Walter (1696–1725) and John Tufts (1689–1750).

"Singing is reducible to the rules of Art," Walter pleaded in *The Grounds and Rules of Musick Explained*, published by James Franklin in 1721. In his pioneer book of instruction in singing the psalms, Walter assured his readers that anyone who would master these rules could sing at sight tunes he had never heard, just as one who knows the rules of reading can read any new book. "This is a Truth," he wrote, anticipating incredulity, "although known to, and proved by many of us, yet very hardly to be received and credited in the country."

John Tufts tried to avoid the problem of notes altogether, offering instead instruction in an original method "of singing by letters instead of notes" in *An Introduction to the Singing of Psalm-Tunes, in a Plain and Easy Method* (which was in print in 1721, and perhaps earlier). This was only the first time Yankee ingenuity attacked the problem of making music simple; efforts of later New England singing masters would meet with greater success than Tufts did.

Walter's *Grounds and Rules*, in any case, met the problem squarely. It promised "an introduction to the Art of Singing by Note, fitted to the meanest capacities," and it came with a prefatory recommendation signed by Increase and Cotton Mather (Walter's grandfather and uncle) and thirteen other ministers.

First Encounters

That so much persuasion was considered necessary suggests that instruction in singing was meeting resistance from laymen. Indeed, the notion of singing schools, on the surface so simple and practical, roused a protest both strong and persistent, especially from old-timers who enjoyed having their own way with the psalms. The reformers regarded the prevalent confusion in psalmsinging as in offense against God—but so, countered the opposition, was mere formality. A writer in the *New England Chronicle* voiced the objection clearly in 1723:

Truly I have a great jealousy that if we once begin to sing by rule, the next thing will be to pray by rule, and preach by rule; and then comes popery.

Influential voices, however, strongly advocated the reform the singing schools proposed to bring about. In a tract called *The Accomplished Singer* (1721), Cotton Mather declared that Heaven would be pleased were "the Congregations, wherein 'tis wanting, to recover a Regular Singing."

We ought certainly to serve our God with our *Best*, and *Regular Singing* must needs be *Better* than the confused Noise of a Wilderness. God is not for Confusion in the Churches of the Saints; but requires, Let all things be done decently.

Thus the heirs of the Puritans pleaded their musical case, hoping against all odds to restore psalmody to its earlier state. Thomas Symmes (1677–1725), like Tufts and Walter a Harvard-trained minister, was especially clear in his expression of their goals. In his *Reasonableness of Regular Singing* (1720) he argued that the "usual way" of singing in the churches— every man for himself, by heart—was a corruption of the "regular" way, "which is the only scriptural good old way of singing; much older than our fathers, or our fathers' grandfathers." And not only did he urge that the singing of the psalms could be promoted "if singing schools were promoted"; he also suggested that this would help cope with a problem beyond that of decorum in church. Does not such a school, he asked, afford also "an innocent and profitable recreation?"

Has it not a tendency to divert young people, who are most proper to learn, from learning *idle, foolish,* yea *pernicious songs and ballads,* and banish all such *trash* from their minds? Experience proves this.

So the schools were instituted, and with the urging of the ministers they were made to thrive. But as with so many of the institutions the Puritans devised, history took the singing school out of their hands and created of it something quite other than they had intended. Their conservative designs had revolutionary consequences. Their attempt to purify and discipline the singing of the psalms resulted in an opportunity for musical activity the community could enjoy outside the church's direct authority.

Though ministers themselves may have conducted the first singing classes, anyone among the settlers who had some practical skill in music now had a chance to make use of it. Singing teachers were so few and congregations so scattered that each teacher had to divide his efforts among a number of communities. The peripatetic singing master thus came into being, carrying his pitchpipe and songbook from settlement to settlement. Independent of the clergy, he organized his own classes, taught them of evenings (he likely was a tradesman by day), and collected his modest fees.

As the singing schools began to catch on, it became increasingly plain that their appeal lay less in the reform of psalmody than in the "innocent and profitable recreation" they offered the colonials, along with cornhuskings and spinning bees. By the time of the Revolution, singing schools had sprung up throughout the colonies. Note was taken of them in Charleston in 1730, in New York in 1754, in Pennsylvania in 1757, as far west as Cincinnati by the turn of the century. The schools grew in number, and the singing teachers began to publish songbooks for their classes; like the English songbooks of the time, these include secular glees and catches along with a share of hymns and anthems that increased as the share of the old psalms diminished.

The singing school thus failed to lead the flock back into the paths of pure psalmody, but it gave rise to the first American music books and to a number of pioneer American composers. John Tufts and Thomas Walter included tunes of their own in their books, and so did Josiah Flagg, whose *Collection of the Best Psalm Tunes* (1764), "the greater part of them never before printed in America," is recorded as the first publication engraved by Paul Revere and printed on paper made in British America. James Lyon (1735–94) of Philadelphia produced in *Urania* (1761) the first collection of hymns and psalm tunes made by a native American, some of the music being Lyon's own.

The most memorable of the singing teachers, William Billings (1746–1800), produced in 1770 *The New-England Psalm-Singer*, a collection of his psalms, anthems, and "fuging tunes." The latter were compositions in a form for which Billings had great enthusiasm; though far from being thoroughly worked out fugues, they did bring the various voices into play one after the other, singing the same notes with a canonic effect sometimes rough but also rugged and lively.

Born in Boston and a tanner by trade, Billings was a self-taught musican of enormous zest. He early struck a note of individualism in American music that was rarely to find an echo before Charles Ives's music in our own century. "Nature is the best Dictator," said Billings,

13

. . . for all the hard, dry studied rules that ever was prescribed, will not enable any person to form an air. . . . I don't think myself confin'd to any rules, for composition, laid down by any that went before me . . . ; so in fact, I think it best for every *Composer* to be his own *Carver.*

Some of the music in William Billings's half-dozen tune books had, indeed, a freshness and vigor that set it above the work of his many psalm-tune- and anthem-writing contemporaries. Even more appealing and more precious than the music itself, however, was the hardy, enthusiastic, original spirit of the man. He was the musical embodiment of Crèvecoeur's "new man—the American." And his work was far removed from the purified psalmody that John Tufts, Thomas Walter, Cotton Mather, and Thomas Symmes had in mind when two generations earlier they had urged the formation of singing schools.

In the church itself, the schools did not merely reform congregational singing, they led to the acceptance of choirs. "The singers," as the singing-school groups were called, came to occupy a special place in many meeting houses. Having practiced their psalms and hymns carefully, they were soon impatient with the tedious practice of lining out, and pressed to sing the music straight through from start to finish.

Resistance to the idea of the choir was as stubborn as resistance to the schools had been, and the controversy continued long. As late as 1771, John Adams wrote in his diary of the singing in an old church he had visited, "It is the *old way*, as we call it—all the drawling, quavering discord in the world." And in 1779, when the congregation in Worcester, Massachusetts, voted to establish "the singers" in the gallery to "carry on the singing in public worship," the church's aging deacon made a last, sad, vain attempt to perform his time-honored office of giving out the hymn line by line. The choir simply sang him down, the story goes, and his "attempt to resist the progress of improvement" thus overpowered, the old man left the meeting house in tears. The full implications of the irresistible "progress of improvement" were to be realized only as the eighteenth passed into the nineteenth century. Puritan psalmody's encounter with New England life had produced the singing school. From the schools arose pioneer American music books and composers, and later would come musical clubs, choral societies, public school music, and full-fledged conservatories. The singing school as a force was only beginning to be felt; it was to have some surprisingly productive encounters with other forces as it made its way in the growing cities, in the frontier settlements of the West, and among the Negro slaves in the South.

II

Ardent Amateurs,
Venturesome Professionals

Because it was a subject of controversy, we have a fair record of the part of colonial American musical practice that centered about psalm-singing and the development of singing schools. On the rest we can only speculate or make deductions from scanty evidence. Other kinds of music-making could have been so commonplace no one troubled to write about them at the time. John Cotton, in 1647, granted that "any private Christian who hath a gifte to frame a spirituall song" might not only compose and sing it but might also play it on a musical instrument, provided that "the instrument does not divert the heart from attention to the matter of the song." But to what extent the Puritans of New England made instrumental music at home, and in what forms, is not known.

Of professional musical performance there seems to have been almost none until well into the eighteenth century. Governor

Amateurs and Professionals

John Leverett wrote home from Boston in 1673 that there was "not a Musician in the Colony," and if he meant professional musician it was very likely true. As late as 1714, when after much discussion an organ imported three years earlier by Thomas Brattle was installed in Boston's King's Chapel, an organist had to be brought from England "to play skilfully thereon with a loud noise." The religious music of certain German pietist sects in Pennsylvania at the end of the seventeenth century, like the concert music of the Moravian Brethren in Bethlehem in the 1740's, was a remarkable exception.

The growth of cities, the increasing secularization of American life, and continuing waves of immigration changed the picture completely in the new century. Ardent musical amateurs were joined by immigrant professional musicians, and musical activity gradually broadened to include musical theater. The arrival of English opera on the American scene was another of those crucial meetings that marked the course of the country's musical history.

The English opera—ballad opera—crossed the Atlantic with the commerce and emigration set in motion by the Treaty of Utrecht. The America that received it was remarkably different from that which had received Puritan psalmody a century earlier. With the influx of immigrants beginning with the peace of 1713, the population of the colonies quadrupled in the ensuing fifty years. The newcomers were not all English; they were French, German, and above all Scotch-Irish. The increasing diversity and dispersion of the population along with growing commerce and prosperity furthered the secularization of eighteenth-century American society.

The earliest newspaper, Boston's weekly *News Letter*, carried the first surviving notice of a public concert: the issue of December 16–23, 1731, advertised "a concert of music on sundry instruments in Mr. Pelham's great Room" to take place on December 30. Concerts may well have been given earlier in Boston and elsewhere. Indeed, the first issue of the *South Carolina Gazette*, in 1732, announced concerts, organ recitals, and other musical performances in a tone that suggests they were already an accepted part of Charles Town life. Although mention of concerts is scattered and rare in the earliest American newspapers, concerts, public as well as private, were very likely being given in American colonial cities before the 1730's. Means other than newspapers existed to make them known to those interested. In any case, records of early performances are so scant that even that meticulous researcher, Oscar G. Sonneck, could only speculate as to what the first American concertgoers listened to—"more or less skillful renditions of Corelli, Vivaldi, Purcell, Abaco, Handel, Geminiani and other such masters whose fame was firmly established in Europe."

If the colonies could boast anything like a music center at this point, it was Charles Town (it became Charleston after the Revolution). From the 1730's at least, South Carolina's rice- and indigo-rich society patronized annual subscription balls arranged for them by local music and dancing masters. Concerts—followed, as was the British custom of the time, by "country dances for the diversion of the ladies"—had a place alongside balls, horse races, and cockfights among the favorite amusements of the prosperous Charles Town folk and the neighboring planters, who brought their families with them to the city for the festive winter season.

Charles Town had a population of less than seven thousand in 1742, and more than half of that number were slaves. Yet the city's zest for the music English society enjoyed attracted mu-

Amateurs and Professionals

sicians from the northern colonies and from Europe. Thus Charles Theodor Pachelbel (1690–1750), son of an eminent German composer, ventured in 1730 to Boston and then made his way from a church organist's job in Rhode Island, by way of benefit concerts in New York, down to Charles Town, where he spent the last thirteen years of his life.

Other professional musicians were similarly drawn by Charles Town's lively culture, which took on a special flavor through the influence of the West Indies and of Huguenot immigrants. There Pachelbel and his colleagues gave lessons in harpsichord, violin, guitar, flute, and cello, with the consequence that in 1762 Charles Town musical amateurs were able to form a St. Cecilia Society, the earliest organization of its kind to achieve any sort of permanence in America. The club supported an orchestra of paid musicians who, with the help of local amateur performers, gave concerts fortnightly for 120 members and their friends.

By this time, New York and Boston enjoyed subscription concerts. Even in Philadelphia, where pressure of Quaker disapproval restricted musical activity a little longer to private affairs, a series of concerts was offered for public subscription in 1764. But the number of professional musicians in the colonies was still small. Private concerts could not offer skilled performances by trained musicians such as the English or European gentry enjoyed in their salons. The American musician, where he appeared, was an amateur; the professional, most often a newly arrived German, Frenchman, or Englishman, needed the assistance of "private gentlemen" to bring together an ensemble for a public performance.

Benjamin Franklin was able to accept the low estate of the colonies' music as a necessity. "Agriculture and the mechanic arts" were of the most immediate importance, he wrote in 1749. "The culture of minds by the finer arts and sciences" would have to be postponed to "times of more wealth and leisure." He himself, however, took a lively interest in music, wrote about it in terms both thoughtful and original, and even applied his inventiveness to it.

About 1760 in London, he heard a performance on a set of musical glasses filled with water and set in harmonious vibration by the touch of a virtuoso's fingertips to the rims. Charmed "by the sweetness of its tones and the music . . . produced from it," Franklin wished that the set of glasses might be arranged in a more convenient form "and brought together in a narrower compass, so as to admit of a greater number of tones, and all within reach of hand to a person sitting before the instrument."

By 1762 "the celebrated Glassy-chord, invented by Mr. Franklin of Philadelphia" was delighting British audiences. In the next decades the new instrument, commonly called the glass harmonica or simply harmonica, was heard with widespread admiration on the Continent and elicited compositions from Mozart and Beethoven, among others. In Philadelphia, Franklin's highly musical young friend, Francis Hopkinson, set himself the task of improving the instrument by applying a keyboard to it, a project the youthful Thomas Jefferson thought would be (if successful) "the greatest present which has been made to the musical world this century, not excepting the Piano-forte."

Jefferson himself was the most passionate of musical amateurs. As a law student in Williamsburg in the 1760's, he won the friendship of Governor Francis Fauquier, who indulged his own love for music with weekly concerts in the governor's palace. The young Jefferson not only enjoyed the "Attic societies" of the governor's dinners, but, as violinist, happily joined Fauquier

Amateurs and Professionals

"and two or three other amateurs" in the weekly performances, with music of Handel, Tartini, and Christian Bach likely featured in the repertoire.

In the following decade, when Jefferson left Williamsburg for his newly built home in the frontier county of Albemarle, he ordered a German clavichord as a special gift for the bride he would take with him. Then he saw for the first time a newly developed instrument that was gaining attention in Europe, the "pianoforte," and was charmed by it into changing his mind. Fastidious, knowledgeable, and well-to-do, he sent (to London) for a piano "of fine mahogany, solid, not vineered. The compass from Double G. to F. in alt. a plenty of spare strings; and the workmanship of the whole very handsome, and worthy the acceptance of a lady for whom I intend it."

Jefferson's musical appetites were too aristocratic for satisfaction in the American setting. He is pictured as an inveterate hummer of minuets and an avid parlor violinist—"the finest unprofessional player" ever heard by a British captain who had an opportunity to play duets with him when, as one of a group of Revolutionary War prisoners interned at Charlottesville, he occasionally enjoyed the Jeffersons' hospitality at Monticello.

Jefferson wrote in 1778 to an acquaintance in France, bewailing America's meager musical resources and outlining a wistful plan which evidently he was able to carry no further:

The bounds of an American fortune will not admit the indulgence of a domestic band of musicians, yet I have thought that a passion for music might be reconciled with that economy which we are obliged to observe. I retain among my domestic servants a gardener, a weaver, a cabinet-maker and a stone-cutter, to which I would add a *vigneron*. In a country where, like yours, music is cultivated and practiced by every class of men, I suppose there might be found persons of these trades who could perform on the French horn, clarinet or hautboy, and bassoon, so that one might have a band of two French horns, two clarinets, two hautboys and a bassoon, without enlarging their domestic expense.

John Adams was able to view the young land's musical deficiencies more philosophically than Jefferson. Writing from Paris in 1780, he noted how easily an American might be carried away by the musical and other aesthetic delights there, but reasoned,

My duty is to study the science of government that my sons may have the liberty to study mathematics and science. My sons ought to study geography, navigation, commerce, and agriculture in order to give their children a right to study philosophy, painting, poetry, music, architecture, sculpture, tapestry, and porcelain.

Of the musically inclined Founding Fathers, Francis Hopkinson (1737–91) remains the one best remembered as a musician, the most memorable of the eighteenth century's musical amateurs. Poet and pamphleteer of the Revolution, a signer of the Declaration of Independence, treasurer of loans for the wartime Congress, judge of the Admiralty Court of Pennsylvania, Hopkinson was at the same time a prime moving force in Philadelphia's just-beginning musical life. He was instrumental in arranging the city's first public subscription concerts, in which he took part as harpsichordist. And when in 1788 he dedicated his *Seven Songs for the Harpsichord or Forte Piano* to George Washington, he claimed for himself "the credit of being the first native of the United States who has produced a musical Composition."

Hopkinson was a conscious pioneer in the modern role of the secular musical artist, and like the other Founding Fathers he looked upon his work not so much with vanity as with hope that it might signify something for the future. "If this attempt should

Amateurs and Professionals

not be too severely treated," he wrote in the preface to his songs, "others may be encouraged to venture on a path, yet untrodden in America, and the Arts in succession will take root and flourish among us."

In their efforts to establish the art of music in the country, America's early amateurs were aided by a few venturesome professional musicians who crossed the Atlantic to try their fortunes in the British colonies. Public musical performances were only just coming into fashion in London and the European capitals as the eighteenth century began, and the profession of concert manager was a new one. In America, the newcomers not only arranged concerts, they appeared in them as performers, often playing music of their own composition with their pupils as assisting artists.

Such was James Bremner (d. 1780), a Scotsman who began teaching in Philadelphia in 1763, with Francis Hopkinson among his pupils. He and Hopkinson worked together in presenting Philadelphia's first subscription concerts in 1764—nineteen Thursday evenings for the sum of three pounds, which secured the subscriber's admission plus "one Lady's Ticket, to be disposed of every Concert Night, as he thinks proper." The partnership of professional and amateur was mutually beneficial. If Bremner gave Hopkinson and his fellow enthusiasts the satisfaction of professional musical instruction and opportunities to perform in public, the support of such distinguished Philadelphians undoubtedly helped to win respectability for early concerts in the colonies' largest city (population in 1760, 23,750). The pioneer work of Bremner and his generation prepared the way for the next—for men like Alexander Reinagle (1756–1809) (piano teacher to Nelly Custis, George Washington's adopted daughter) and Benjamin Carr (1768–1831) in Philadel-

phia, James Hewitt (1770–1827) in New York, Gottlieb Graupner (1767–1836) in Boston.

"ENTERTAINMENTS OF SINGING"

Despite the colonies' increasing worldliness, theatrical performances were still widely considered an intolerable frivolity.
Philadelphia tried to ban them and Boston succeeded in doing
just that almost to the end of the century. But the southern
cities were less hidebound. Williamsburg may have had a theater
as early as 1716, and it certainly had one by 1722. In the following decade, Charles Town and New York had theaters too.
Since theater and music were virtually inseparable at the time,
these stages perhaps offered musical entertainments from the
beginning, though there is no record of them. On February 8,
1735, however, Charles Town's *South Carolina Gazette* carried
an historic announcement:

On Tuesday the 18th inst. will be presented at the Courtroom the
opera of 'Flora, or Hob in the Well,' with the dance of the two
Pierrots and a new Pantomime entertainment, called the Adventures of Harlequin Scaramouch.

Thus was an opera performance noted for the first time in the
American press. But more historic than the mere notice was the
nature of the thing announced: ballad opera.

The great fashion of London musical theater at this time was
the Italian opera, with mythological plots the vehicles for elaborate stage spectacle and vocal gymnastics of fabled male sopranos
and altos. In the third decade of the century, the emerging London public began to show impatience with these entertainments.
The Spectator chided the opera and its fashionable audience for
pretentiousness, artifice, outlandishness, and plain silliness. In
1728, the protest took musical form: in *The Beggar's Opera*, John

Amateurs and Professionals

Gay put London's rabble on the stage, speaking and singing their own English, in place of the gods of antiquity, and John Christopher Pepusch set Gay's verses to the tunes of popular songs. Thus the ballad opera came into being. In a quarter of a century, *The Beggar's Opera* and its progeny pushed the Italian opera off the London stage.

In America the protest was enjoyed without the provocation. Though the prospering planters and merchants of Charles Town and Williamsburg sought the pleasures of fashionable London, they did not go so far as to import the Italian opera. Not only did they lack theaters equipped for the complicated operatic spectacles; they were untouched by the experience of travel or study on the Continent, which had whetted London appetites for the Italian fare. An exotic entertainment in any setting, the opera of Handel, Jomelli, Buononcini, and their like was simply unimaginable in early America.

Ballad opera, on the other hand, was made to order for the colonial American situation. Easily staged with minimum means, the entertainment's demands were easily met by both players and audience. The audience had the diversion it craved, spoken and sung in its own everyday language, to music often familiar and always hummable. While the situations portrayed, whether urban or pastoral, were unlike anything in America, they gave Americans a pleasant feeling of their own superior well-being. And at the same time, the audience could feel it was enjoying London's latest vogue. Thus while the appearance of the ballad opera in London signified a sharp line drawn between the fashionable and the popular, its appearance in the American colonies signified just the contrary: here the fashionable and the popular were the same.

The early history of the musical theater in America is identical with that of the stage itself. Players were also singers, tragedians were comedians, and dramatic entertainment scarcely existed except in company with musical entertainment. As theaters began to appear in American cities in the second quarter of the eighteenth century, the itinerant "companies of comedians" for whom they were put up unquestionably seasoned their plays with "entertainments of singing." Among them were the ballad operas.

Again, records are scant and yield only hints of the names of players, their repertoire, their itineraries. But there is some evidence: the company of Kean and Murray took the trouble to advertise in the *New York Gazette* their weekly performances in the newly fitted "Theater in Nassau Street" in 1750 and 1751; they gave about a dozen plays (including a version of *The Tragedy of King Richard III*) and as many farces, which were given as after-pieces. Among the latter were ballad operas and the English comic operas which shared their popular style but looked beyond popular songs for their musical material: Fielding's *Mock Doctor*, Hill's *The Devil to Pay*, Cibber's *Damon and Phillida*, the pastoral sketch *Colin and Phoebe*, *Flora, or Hob in the Well*, and in its first performance of record in America, *The Beggar's Opera* itself, given December 3, 1750.

The "New York Company of Comedians" and the "Virginia Company of Comedians" gave similar performances at Annapolis and Williamsburg, probably using the harpsichord for musical accompaniments. When the "Company of Comedians from Annapolis" ventured to Upper Marlborough, Maryland, to open a new theater there in 1752, they performed *The Beggar's Opera* "with Instrumental Music to each Air, given by a Set of Private Gentlemen." It was the first time on record that an opera was performed in America with orchestral accompaniment, thanks to the ever-ready musical amateurs.

But the real beginning of musical theater in America came with the arrival at Yorktown in 1752 of Hallam's London Company of Comedians. A well-organized troupe with its own musicians, the company played the gamut of dramatic and lyric theater from *The Merchant of Venice* to *The Beggar's Opera*, at a higher standard of professionalism than had previously been known in the colonies. In the next two years it made its way from Williamsburg through Annapolis and smaller cities up to New York and Philadelphia. Unfortunately for the Hallam company, Philadelphia in 1754 still shied from the theater. Lewis Hallam had taken precautions; he had secured in advance the support of influential citizens, who were assured that the performances would offend no one's sense of decency. But the moral opposition was too strong. The season was a failure. Hallam and company limped down to worldly Charles Town to recoup, and then embarked for Jamaica.

There Lewis Hallam died, but not his company. Mrs. Hallam married David Douglass, a skilled actor and sound businessman. With Douglass as manager, the London Company returned to New York in 1758 and there "acted with great applause, to a most crowded audience." The troupe then held the stage, traveling the length of the seaboard, until the first Continental Congress, bracing the colonies for the impending struggle against British rule, resolved "that we will discourage every species of extravagance and dissipation, especially horse-racing, and all kinds of gaming, cock-fighting, exhibition of shows, plays and other expensive diversions and entertainments."

By that time, Douglass and his company—now dubbed the

American Music

American Company—had played in Charles Town, Annapolis, Baltimore, Williamsburg, Upper Marlborough, Newport, Providence, Albany, and even fateful Philadelphia, where in 1769 a good long season was possible despite heckling and insults from some who would not abide "the return of those strolling Comedians, who are travelling thro' America, propagating vice and immorality."

The "private gentlemen" who filled out the orchestra for these performances not only were musically helpful, they were in the front line of the battle to make musical theater possible in Philadelphia. This, and not the likelihood of a wrong note or two, must have been what prompted Benjamin Franklin's *Pennsylvania Gazette* to admonish its readers that "The Orchestra, on Opera Nights, will be assisted by some musical persons, who, as they have no View but to contribute to the Entertainment of the Public, certainly claim a Protection from any Manner of Insult."

Not even Boston was proof against the ballad opera. Though stage plays were forbidden there, no law prevented their being read and sung in concerts. David Douglass billed the performances as "Moral Lectures," and *The Beggar's Opera* penetrated New England.

A FEDERAL MUSE

The mood of the colonies was changing, however. Where earlier "blue laws" had been blinked and evaded, Congress's resolution of 1774 discouraging plays and entertainments met with spontaneous sympathy from the public. The American Company of Comedians again set sail for the West Indies as patriots lost their taste for such patently British entertainments and began to savor the martial measures of liberty songs and Revolutionary ballads. Except in Tory strongholds and among the British forces, concerts, plays, and operas were virtually forsworn until the war had come and gone.

Signaling the new mood, William Billings took the hymn "Chester" from his *New-England Psalm-Singer* and gave it the words which made it a rallying song for Washington's troops. And when British soldiers marched out of Boston toward Lexington singing a ditty meant to ridicule American upstarts, the patriots who met them with gunfire took "Yankee Doodle" proudly for their own. Exactly where the tune came from is not clear; it could well have sprung up in America. In any case, the saucy strain of "Yankee Doodle" and Billings's sturdy "Chester" set the cadence of the colonies' march to independence.

Francis Hopkinson lampooned the British in his ballad of "The Battle of the Kegs," which was widely sung after its publication in the *Pennsylvania Packet*, March 4, 1778, though to what tune is not known. Under the more solemn title of an "oratorial entertainment," Hopkinson also wrote both the libretto and the music (now lost) of what some consider the first American attempt at opera, *The Temple of Minerva*. The work, celebrating France's alliance with the United States, was performed in November 1781 before a private gathering at the hotel of the French minister in Philadelphia. There General Washington heard a "band of Gentlemen and Ladies" sing Hopkinson's prophecy of the "future happy state" of Columbia, who "with France in friendship join'd, shall opposing pow'rs defy."

At the war's end, as concert and theater activity began gradually to revive, the alliance with France had musical consequences. French musicians came into the country in fresh numbers, and music of Gretry, Gluck, and Pleyel, favored in Paris at the time, sometimes usurped the place of English and German composers on concert programs.

But the change taking place in American musical life was not merely a shift from British to French influence. What had been musically as otherwise a British colony was now asserting its musical independence. The victorious Americans' patriotism and pride echoed in militia bands parading to marches named for General Washington, along with "Yankee Doodle" and "Chester." Ratification of the Constitution and preparations for Washington's inauguration brought an outpouring of poems and odes printed up as broadsides and sung to well-known melodies ranging from hymn tunes to the popular "To Anacreon in Heaven" (which probably had come over from England in the early days of the war and was later to become "The Star-Spangled Banner"). There were, besides, countless rewordings of "God Save the King"—for instance, "God Save Great Washington" or "God Save the Thirteen States." New Hampshire, the decisive ninth state to ratify the Constitution, celebrated with a "grand procession" in which one float carried a printing press newly invented by Benjamin Dearborn and dubbed the American press. It was in operation all during the parade, striking off "Songs in Celebration of the Ratification of the Federal Constitution" for distribution among the surrounding crowds.

One ardent Boston Federalist seized on "Yankee Doodle" as a vehicle for verses celebrating Massachusetts's ratification of the Constitution. He wrote a stanza for each of the former colonies and then buried the bones of national contention in a final one:

> So here I end my Fed'ral song
> Composed of thirteen verses;
> May agriculture flourish long

Amateurs and Professionals

And commerce fill our purses!
Yankee Doodle, etc.

Francis Hopkinson, who could have written his own tune, preferred to express his sentiments in measures everyone would know how to sing. So his "The New Roof," which he subtitled "A New Song for Federal Mechanics," was set to "To Anacreon in Heaven," with a refrain on this theme:

For our roof we will raise, and our song still shall be
A government firm, and our citizens free.

Concerts were widely used to mark patriotic occasions. One given by the Urania Academy in Philadelphia a few weeks before the Constitutional Convention may be taken as typical. It included the overture of Dr. Arne's *Artaxerxes* and the "Hallelujah!" from Handel's *Messiah*, but also a flute concerto by one Chevalier du Poinceau and works of four Americans: William Billings's anthem "The Rose of Sharon," an "Ode to Friendship" by James Lyon, a setting of the ninety-seventh psalm by William Tuckey of New York, and a violin concerto by Philip Phile. Tuckey (1708–81), an English-born musician, contributed to the development of choral singing in New York and conducted the first American performance of parts of *Messiah* there in 1770. Phile (d. 1793) was later to compose—possibly for Washington's inauguration—a "President's March" familiar today as "Hail, Columbia," the present verses set to it by Francis Hopkinson's son Joseph.

Professional musicians still were at a premium when President Washington visited Boston during his inaugural tour, in October of 1789. A concert given in his honor benefited by the professional capacities of William Selby as organist, composer, and conductor, the efforts of "a society of gentlemen," and "the

31

band of His Most Christian Majesty's Fleet"—meaning the French. But the shortage was gradually being remedied. The ban on theatrical entertainment was lifted, and brighter prospects, plus troubled times abroad, brought professional musicians to the new Republic not only from France but also from England and Germany.

The Old American Company ventured back to Philadelphia and New York in 1784, and within a decade it had competition: in Philadelphia the comedian Thomas Wignell formed a theatrical company with Alexander Reinagle, recently arrived from England, as musical director; and in 1790 there arrived at Baltimore the first of several groups of French players, refugees from France and Santo Domingo, who in the next half-dozen years brought a first taste of French opera and concert music to New York, Philadelphia, Boston, and Charleston.

But it remained for the Old American Company itself to take the turn toward American music as it was to be. In 1787, Lewis Hallam, Jr., and his partner John Henry had offered New York audiences the first professionally performed comedy by an American author: Royall Tyler's *The Contrast*. The prologue, spoken by the same Thomas Wignell later associated with Reinagle, voiced the temper of the times:

> Why should our thoughts to distant countries roam,
> When each refinement may be found at home? . . .
> Strange! we should thus our native worth disclaim,
> And check the progress of our rising fame.

Within a decade, the same spirit spurred the company to venture the first considerable American opera. Musical entertainment in general had returned to the theater more slowly than straight plays, but after a cautionary period during which the subterfuge of "moral lectures" again prevailed, the English

Amateurs and Professionals

comic opera once more held the stage. There was a new mood in the land, however, and the Old American Company's new manager, William L. Dunlap (the first historian of the American theater), sensed it and responded. The result was *The Archers, or The Mountaineers of Switzerland*, with music by Benjamin Carr, who was already eminent in Philadelphia as music dealer, publisher, and composer-performer.

The Archers was written in ballad-opera style and based on the William Tell legend, but in Dunlap's libretto, the Swiss revolt of 1315 against Austrian domination was made to speak directly to Americans:

> Let every act, let every thought
> Be center'd in our country's good:
> Just laws are not too dearly bought
> Though purchased with our dearest blood.

The New York *Diary* caught the patriotic spirit of both the opera and the moment in an ardent review of the first performance, at the John Street Theater April 18, 1796:

This opera is the production of an American citizen, and as such should meet the patronage of the public . . . . We have too long been accustomed to look up to England, as the source of our theatrical entertainments . . . . The most paltry importations of ribaldry and nonsense are too apt to pass for sense and wit; . . . whilst the productions of the American muse are disregarded because they are not foreign . . . . Is it not time that this evil should be remedied?

The Archers was further lauded for expressing "those principles which we hope will ever be dear to us," "that sentiment which must ever inspire freemen with a sense of their rights and a will to preserve them." The dissatisfaction with opera imported from England was explicit: it ridiculed vices nonexistent in America, said the *Diary*. "The modern English plays are not applicable to this country."

33

American Music

Dunlap's libretto and two ingratiating numbers from Carr's score are all that remain to us of *The Archers*. But clearly it answered an incipient yearning for some identifiable American artistic expression, and clearly it offered hope that such a thing as an "American muse" might actually exist. Tyler's *Contrast* included one vignette humorously suggestive of what was generally held to be the state of American musical culture at the time. When his Yankee Jonathan is asked to sing a song, he confesses, "Why, all my tunes are go to meeting tunes, save one," that one being, of course, "Yankee Doodle." As the young United States moved toward the nineteenth century, it appeared that this was going to change. Something new was about to appear, and both the "go to meeting tunes" and the English opera were leading to it.

Again history afforded a period of gestation. As the century turned, immigration dwindled under the pressure of British emigration restrictions and the disruption of shipping during the Napoleonic Wars. The new country and its new citizens stirred by feelings of nationalism were again thrown on their own resources for indigenous solutions to indigenous problems. Before, the seaboard centers of culture had opened themselves eastward toward Europe. Now the West was to be heard from, and the Negro.

III

Frontier Voices

The theater was an amusement of the towns, but that meant only a small part of the American people. Of the 5,308,483 Americans counted in the census of 1800, 95 per cent lived outside the cities. Timothy Dwight, traveling through New England, found the country people enjoying "visiting, dancing, music, conversation, walking, riding, sailing, shooting at a mark, draughts (checkers), chess." Outside New England he could have added horse racing and cockfighting, and toward the mountains—which half a million Americans now had crossed—barn-raisings and husking bees.

Musically, the singing school was the center of activity, though Jonathan of *The Contrast* probably was less than candid in claiming to know only go-to-meeting tunes and "Yankee Doodle." Old English ballads had endured in the colonies, and the immigrant Scots and Scotch-Irish brought fresh music that later generations were to discover as "folksongs." The songs are seldom mentioned in writings of the period, perhaps because they were taken too much for granted. In any case, there were real bars to their being noted. Those who sang such songs, mostly back-country people, were not writing people, and those who wrote, mostly city folk and ministers, deemed the songs less than respectable and better forgotten.

They were sung, however, and many of the tunes served religious as well as secular purposes. When John Wesley came to America in 1735, he was inspired by Moravian companions to a new belief in the power of hymnody. He published his own first hymns at Charles Town in 1737, and after his return to England he wrote more. Like Luther before him, Wesley fitted melodies of familiar songs to religious texts. American back-country people surely had anticipated him. The strict verses of the *Bay Psalm Book* had already given way to the more literary psalms of Nahum Tate and Nicholas Brady, and even the latter had largely been replaced in worshippers' affections by the hymn-poetry of Isaac Watts. To the new textual freedom, the people—with or without John Wesley's sanction—added the license of singing their hymns to tunes they knew.

One of the earliest compilers to write down and publish these folk hymns was Jeremiah Ingalls (1764-1828), in *The Christian Harmony*, printed in New Hampshire in 1805. Ingalls was an innkeeper, bass viol-player, farmer, cooper, deacon of his Vermont church and leader of the local singing school. There is no evidence that he profited from setting down for the first time "the unwritten music in general use" in country congregations. George Pullen Jackson supposes, with reason, that the country people were happy enough with their tuneless word books of "self-selected and home made" hymns which they

Frontier Voices

sang to memorized tunes, and that shunning these backwoods songs, members of the older congregations proudly sang fuguing tunes and anthems by their own singing teachers and other "eminent masters." But Jeremiah Ingalls was only a little ahead of the times. Before the middle of the nineteenth century, at least thirty such books were published, most of them south and west of New England, as religion in the young United States took on a new cast.

The great increase in the population of the colonies between 1713 and 1763 had important effects on American religious life. It increased the sectarianism to which the settlers were already prone, but at the same time it gave rise to a movement toward cooperative action among the separate denominations, to counteract tendencies toward free-thinking in the East and toward "barbarism" in the frontier West. Voluntary societies were formed to carry on evangelical and revival work in the back country where there were no churches. During the Great Awakening before the Revolution and especially during the Great Revival after the Revolution, the country was swept by mass demonstrations of religious fervor that crossed sectarian barriers. The fervor was expressed and communicated in congregational singing; in frontier communities unlettered settlers from the British Isles now took the words of the hymns from the leader's "deaconing" and sang them to melodies their families had known for generations, the melodies of old ballads like "Barbara Allen," "Lord Lovell," "Little Sir Hugh."

At the turn of the century, frontier religion expressed itself in massive camp meetings. There had been outdoor religious meetings before, during the Great Awakening. But in the frontier communities in the southern uplands, and across the mountains in western Pennsylvania, Kentucky, and Tennessee, they took on new dimensions. A meeting would begin on a Thursday and last till the following Tuesday, with singing and praying almost uninterrupted. Settlers came from thirty, sixty, even a hundred miles away in wagons loaded with families and provisions. The wagons served as shelter, along with improvised huts and tents. The spectacular meeting at Cane Ridge, Kentucky, in August 1801 was described by a witness:

I attended with eighteen Presbyterian ministers and Baptist and Methodist preachers, I do not know how many . . . . The number of people computed from ten to twenty-one thousand . . . . Great numbers were on the ground from Friday until the Thursday following, night and day without intermission. . . . They are commonly collected in small circles of ten or twelve, close adjoining another circle and all singing Watts' and Hart's hymns. . . and then a minister steps upon a stump or log and begins an exhortation. . . . One Sabbath night I saw above 100 candles burning at once and I saw I suppose 100 persons at once on the ground crying for mercy, of all ages from eight to sixty years. . . . When a person is struck down he is carried by others out of the congregation, when some minister converses with, and prays for him; afterwards a few gather around and sing hymns suitable to his case.

A present-day descendant of Bishop Francis Asbury, one of the first Methodist circuit riders, has described the spiritual singing of the old camp meeting, as it was communicated to him by his grandparents, and as it survives in camp meetings in the South:

There was no instrument, not even the tuning fork. . . . Some brass-lunged relative of mine pitched the tune. If he pitched it in the skies, no matter. The men singing the leading part with him were as brass-lunged as he. As for the women, they placed an octave over the men's leading part, singing around high C with perfect unconcern because they didn't realize their feat. The immediate din was tremendous; at a hundred yards it was beautiful; at a distance of half a mile it was magnificent.

Frontier Voices

The traveling singing-school teachers and the revival song leaders soon began to provide tune books and manuals for the frontier meetings. The new books kept the format of their predecessors, the books of William Billings, Thomas Walter, and John Tufts. Printed on oblong pages about twice as wide as high, they began with "an easy introduction to the rudiments of music," often including secular glees and catches for singing-school use; then came the hymns, odes, psalms, fuguing tunes, and anthems for congregational use. The new books differed from the old, however, in two important ways: the tunes selected included a large share of folk hymns, the "unwritten music," the "southern" or "western melodies" already in common use but previously unprinted; and the musical instruction introduced a new, simplified system of "shape notes" through which those unable to read conventional musical notation could learn to sing unfamiliar tunes with comparative ease.

The most widely adopted shape note method was invented by William Little and William Smith of Albany, who published it in *The Easy Instructor* in 1801, and possibly earlier. A different system of shape notes, dispensing with the musical staff altogether, was advanced by Andrew Law of Connecticut in his *Musical Primer* of 1803, but like John Tufts's letter-notation three generations earlier, it failed to gain acceptance. The Little and Smith method was to name the seven notes of the ordinary scale, using just four different note names; the first three—faw, sol, and law—were repeated for the next three notes, and the seventh was called mi. When a tune was written on the musical staff, its notes were given different shapes according to their names: a triangle for faw, circle for sol, square for law, diamond for mi. Just these four shape notes sufficed for writing the tunes in general use, even for the straightforward bass and treble parts added to them by the tune-book compilers.

The method of Little and Smith caught on and prospered. Indeed, it continued to prosper in the mid-twentieth century, for a version of *The Sacred Harp* shape-note song book, first published in 1844, remains in wide use in rural southern churches and even in a few northern big-city churches where southern-born members still like to learn their hymns "by the notes."

Benjamin Franklin White of Spartanburg, South Carolina, who compiled *The Sacred Harp*, included in the song book a number of the folk hymns first published by his brother-in-law William Walker in *The Southern Harmony* in 1835. "Singing Billy" Walker's song book sold 600,000 copies before the Civil War; it was so popular general stores were expected to have it on hand along with groceries and tobacco. In its pages were found "white spirituals," like "Promised Land," along with hymns with tunes adapted from the ballads of "Captain Kidd," "Little Sir Hugh," and others now less familiar but then widely known. Though such music clearly had its origin in the British Isles, its setting in *The Southern Harmony*, *The Sacred Harp*, and other such books had a distinctive American flavor, not least in the compiler's primitive approach to harmony. Following William Billings's injunction, each compiler was "his own carver," heeding only the rules set by his own ear for what would sing easily and sound clearly—beautiful at a hundred yards, magnificent at half a mile.

Such were the hymns that brought the camp meeting to its climax. The old Methodists were not thinking of their singing, Samuel Asbury notes. "What they were there for was to hammer on the sinner's heart and bring him to the mourner's bench." The preachers would exhort, and the congregation would respond,

Frontier Voices

"Amen" from the men, "Glory!" from the women, until at last the leader focused the wave of emotion in the singing of one of the old folk hymns. Then "all the preachers came down out of the pulpit to exhort even louder than the singing," and sinners came "flocking to the mourner's bench, kneeling in the straw . . . praying on each other's backs five deep." An observer at one of the early camp meetings described the moment:

The very clouds seemed to separate and give way to the people of God ascending to the heavens; while thousands of tongues with the sound of hallelujah seemed to roll through infinite space; while hundreds of people lay prostrate on the ground crying for mercy.

NEGRO SPIRITUALS

The religion of the Great Awakening and the Great Revival bridged not only sectarian gaps, but also gaps of geography, language, nationality, and race. And as it reached the Negro slave in the South, and included him, it drew from him a musical expression that has since affected every kind of music identifiable as American.

We know little about musical practice among the Negro slaves during their first century in America. The inhuman conditions under which they were shipped from Africa scarcely permitted their bringing musical instruments with them. During the crossing, the human cargo were sometimes herded upon deck and bidden to dance. This they did, providing release for themselves and entertainment for the sailors; but they accompanied themselves not on African instruments, but on ships' barrels and pots. In America, the slaves managed to improvise drums and other instruments such as the "banjar" (banjo) out of whatever materials they could find. The drums were frowned upon by slave-owners; they might stir excitement and lead to rebellious-

41

ness. But the masters did not fail to note a musical bent among their slaves and turn it to their own purposes. The Negro fiddler was a familiar figure at dancing parties from the seventeenth into the nineteenth century, in the plantation houses, in frontier settlements, in Williamsburg mansions, and even in the North. How much of his own musical accent crept into the Negro's performance of the white man's minuets, reels, and jigs it is impossible to know.

Revivalist religion and its hymns came as a spiritual and emotional boon to the Negro. The Reverend Samuel Davies (later a president of Princeton), leading a Presbyterian mission in the South in 1755, was deeply impressed by the slaves' response to the hymnals that were among religious books sent for his use in Hanover, Virginia:

> The books were all very acceptable, but none more so than the psalms and hymns, which enabled them to gratify their peculiar taste for psalmody. Sundry of them lodged all night in my kitchen and sometimes when I have awaked about two or three o'clock in the morning, a torrent of sacred harmony has poured into my chamber and carried my mind away to heaven. In this exercise some of them spend the whole night.

Thomas Jefferson marked not only musical responsiveness among the Negroes, but possibly musical creativity as well. In his *Notes on the State of Virginia* (1784), Jefferson remarked, "In music they are more generally gifted than the whites, with accurate ears for tune and time, and they have been found capable of imagining a small catch. Whether they will be equal to the composition of a more extensive run of melody, or of complicated harmony, is yet to be proved." As the Negroes increasingly expressed their musical inventiveness in religious song, some of their white coreligionists increasingly doubted the virtue of encouraging them. Charles C. Jones, who chronicled *The Religious Instruction of the Negroes in the United States*, cautioned in 1842 that hymns taught them "should not be intricate but plain and awakening"; "they are thereby induced to lay aside the extravagant and nonsensical chants, and catches and hallelujah songs of their own composing."

A good deal of scholarly effort has been applied in recent years to tracing and sorting the African and Anglo-Saxon antecedents of the Negro spiritual. Ultimately, all research and controversy serve only to intensify wonder at the uniqueness of what was created both in these songs and in the music that followed from them. For they were the product of a peculiar coincidence of forces, influences, circumstances that could not occur in Europe, or in Africa, nor among free Negroes in the American North, but only among the Negro slaves of the American South. Clearly both West African music and Anglo-Saxon hymnody contributed to it. The essence of the Negro spiritual, however, derived from neither, but rather from this people living in this place at this time. What the slaves inherited of West African music, what they learned of Anglo-Saxon hymnody figure in the Negro spiritual much as hydrogen and oxygen figure in water; the process of their combining created something wholly new.

The development of the Negro spiritual extended across nearly a century, from the eve of the Revolution to the eve of the Civil War. In the 1770's, chapels in Virginia and North Carolina were, in the words of contemporary reports, "full of white and black," "hundreds of negroes. . . with tears streaming down their cheeks." Later, as John Hope Franklin has pointed out, Methodist and Baptist camp meetings were "the most effective means of releasing the pent up emotions that the barren life of the rural South created. . . . Under such circumstances, whites and Negroes sang together, shouted together, and spent themselves emotionally together."

Those Negroes who came in increasing numbers to Christianity still shared, in their quarters and at work, the remnants of West African musical practice that survived on the plantation. The two were not so widely separated as they might have appeared to white observers. Modern historians of the spiritual and of jazz have cited important characteristics held in common by the two musics. The "call-and-response" pattern typical of work chants in West Africa was echoed on the American cotton plantations; it was a pattern not dissimilar from the "deaconing" of hymns heard in evangelical churches. The West African tradition of melodic improvisation found new kin in the backwoods hymn singer's persistent tendency to embellish the simple lines of the psalms and hymns. And the emotional pitch of revivalist singing, mounting to ecstasy and hysteria, was shared by the religion the Negro inherited from Africa. Indeed, in the 1780's, Georgia whites were perturbed by the intensity of the Negro's response in Christian meetings; Negro preachers were proscribed and evening meetings were broken up. A decade later the Great Revival swept the restrictions away.

As the nineteenth century began, there occurred with relation to the Negro and hymnody one of those lulls in outside influence which have so often proved creative for American music. The foreign slave trade was legally abolished in 1808, and though the law did not actually end it, it did diminish the flow of the old musical and religious influence directly from West Africa. At the same time, as the slave states braced for a struggle to perpetuate their "peculiar institution," slaves were denied further education and white preachers began—to the Negro's disillusion-

Frontier Voices

ment—to use their pulpits to preach subservience. Now the Negro's hymn singing became less something shared with white men and more something private to him and his people. The verses, subtly changed from their Anglo-Saxon models, took on double meanings in which the themes of salvation, Heaven and Promised Land were also tokens of hoped-for emancipation and freedom. The melodies, no longer so often sung in company of whites, wandered in the direction of the Negro's own musical inheritance.

The survival of West African musical practice among the plantation Negroes was noted long before the Civil War. Planters were apprehensive of the excitement the Negro's religious and dance music seemed to rouse, and they discouraged their slaves from indulging in it. Overseers, however, did not discourage the chanting of work songs, which helped to get the work done. Visitors in the South often were struck by the strange music they heard in the fields, at the docks, or aboard ferries—the vestiges, at least, of West African musical tradition. One such visitor, the English actress Fanny Kemble, caught in the Negro's singing "some resemblance to tunes with which they must have become acquainted through the instrumentality of white men." But at the same time, she heard something "extraordinarily wild and unaccountable," unlike anything she knew. This same something was described in detail eighteen years later, in 1856, by the architect Frederick Law Olmsted. During one of his trips through the South by rail, he was awakened by the singing of a Negro loading gang just outside his car.

Suddenly, one raised such a shout as I had never heard before; a long, loud, musical shout, rising and falling, and breaking into falsetto, his voice ringing through the woods in the clear, frosty night air, like a bugle call. As he finished, the melody was caught up by another, and then, by several in chorus.

American Music

Olmsted must have heard the Negro's "field holler," which John W. Work later described as a "fragmentary bit of yodel, half sung, half yelled." This spontaneous cry of joy or loneliness or oppression was idiomatic among the southern slaves as it was among their West African forebears, and the "wild and unaccountable" flavor of it remained to define the spiritual, blues, and jazz. Even in the days closer to the Revolution, when the Negro first hopefully learned the white man's religion and the white man's songs, some of the quality of the "holler" crept into his singing. Outsiders who heard him were charmed by the half-exotic, half-familiar and often plaintive flavor of his singing. Furthermore, while the spiritual was developing among the Negroes, white Americans were appropriating some of the outward characteristics of the early plantation songs, and of the Negro himself, in order to create a new form for their own entertainment: minstrelsy.

"ETHIOPIAN OPERA"

One is tempted to view minstrelsy simply as the product of English opera's encounter with the music of the plantation Negro. But the derivation of minstrelsy is in fact complex. It is true that several ballad operas imported from England toward the end of the eighteenth century featured Negro roles portrayed by English singing actors. Charles Dibdin's *The Padlock*, perhaps the earliest of these, was given by the American Company in New York in 1769, seven months after it was introduced in London. It is a neat coincidence that the Negro role of Mungo was played by Lewis Hallam, whose father had founded the American Company, and who had a leading role in *The Archers* in 1796 (when *The Padlock*, by the way, was still in the repertoire). The composer of *The Archers*, Benjamin Carr, seems,

Frontier Voices

moreover, to have been the first American to publish (about 1801) a "Negro Song." Since *The Archers* was supposed to point the way for the American theater to free itself from English domination, and since both its composer and one of its stars were connected with "Negro music," the tie would seem to have been clearly made. The real link, however, was more meaningful than these coincidences. It had less to do with English opera itself than with the impact of the frontier on the players and on the theater in general.

As the reception of *The Archers* suggested, the public was vaguely dissatisfied with its imported amusements, particularly with the fashionable fare of English opera. Though the English opera held the stage till the arrival of the first Italian troupe in 1825, it had to fight for its life after the Revolution against the circus, a new form of entertainment aimed at an audience of greater numbers and less sophistication.

In the 1790's, John Ricketts installed his new circus directly opposite the Chestnut Street Theater in Philadelphia. Wignell and Reinagle howled in protest. But they soon were forced to bring a French troupe of pantomimists and acrobats from Charleston to broaden the appeal of their programs of plays, concerts, and operas. The circus, for its part, was pleased to offer some attractions to the theater audience: in addition to equestrians, rope-dancers, tumblers, pantomimes, and "spectacles," it included occasional performances of concert music, plays, and even full-length comic operas. Since the two entertainments clearly were competing for the same audience, the theater was struck a blow in Philadelphia when Ricketts secured exclusive rights to Saturday evening performances. Determined to stay on the stage and widen their following, the players took to the road. Groups of entertainers from Philadelphia, New York,

American Music

Boston, Charleston, Baltimore, and Richmond headed south and west to bring back-country settlements their first taste of theater.

If the urban audience had found that "the modern English plays are not applicable to this country," what were the frontier people to make of them? In an effort to win audiences, the wandering players, haunted even in the countryside by the circus, salted their programs with comic and novelty numbers, with pantomimes and dances. Common among these, at least from the 1820's on, were blackface dances and "plantation songs" which at first were probably excerpted from familiar English operas, and empty of any actual Negro musical character except accompaniment by such Negro instruments as banjo, bones, and tambourine.

A strolling player named Thomas Dartmouth Rice (1808–1860) did just such a dance in Louisville, in 1828 or 1829, but with a new touch of realism. As the story goes, Rice happened to see an old Negro, somewhat lame with rheumatism, at work in a stable near the Louisville theater where Rice at that time was playing the role of a Negro field hand in the current play. To the young entertainer's glee, the old man sang a queer little song to himself, and with every chorus of

> Wheel about and turn about and do jis so,
> Eb'ry time I wheel about I jump Jim Crow,

did an odd little shuffle and jig that gave Tom Rice an idea. He decided to do a Negro dance at intermission, but a new kind, based on the shuffle-hop and song of old Jim Crow. The number was a hit, not only in Louisville, but soon all along the road back to New York. "Daddy" Rice danced in London in 1836, and "Jim Crow" became the first international song hit from America.

48

Frontier Voices

The impersonation earned "Jim Crow" Rice, among all early blackface performers, the title of "Father of American Minstrelsy." His plantation Negro character was soon followed by a city counterpart named "Zip Coon," created either by George Washington Dixon or Bob Farrell (both claimed the honor). As these and other such numbers quickly caught the public fancy, the next logical step was creation of a show completely in blackface. The step was taken early in 1843, when Daniel Decatur Emmett (1815–1904) together with his friends William Whitlock, Richard Pelham, and Frank Brower, somehow hit on the notion of making their band—fiddle, banjo, tambourine, and bones—the basis for an evening-long performance of "Ethiopian scenes." The Virginia Minstrels, as they called themselves, made their debut in a Bowery music hall. And in short order they were so successful that competitors sprang up throughout the country and the world: Christy's Minstrels, Bryant's Minstrels, Alabama Minstrels, Columbia Minstrels, Ethiopian Serenaders, Kentucky Minstrels, Kentucky Rattlers, and so on. The form of entertainment Emmett had concocted was to prevail almost to the end of the century.

In discussing "Negro minstrelsy" it is important to keep in mind that it was mostly the creation of white entertainers who had little awareness of the real nature of the Negro's music. The music of minstrelsy was wholly different from the enduring music created by the Negro himself out of his own experience. Rather, it was an amusing or sentimental amalgam based on the white man's notions of Negro life. The music was drawn mostly from the experience of the strolling players of the early 1800's. As they traveled, they heard what could not be heard in the cities—the songs of boatmen, stage drivers, wagoners, dock hands. It was American backwoods music, and the fact that it

49

was made by people on the move made it a mixture of work songs, banjo and fiddle music, hymn tunes, drinking songs, and whatever else might be heard in the fields, on the wharves, and in the taverns and meeting houses of the new settlements. The Negro element it contained came mainly from the frontier's ubiquitous Negro fiddler and banjo player—that part of Negro musical practice closest to Irish jigs and Scottish reels, farthest from West African tradition.

Brought to the stage and reinterpreted by the minstrel performers, the music sounded new and exotic to city audiences, but its flavor was essentially Anglo-Saxon despite the players' blackface, garb, and dialect. Minstrel troups actually composed of Negroes began to appear in the 1850's, but by then the form and style of the entertainment were fixed; Negro minstrels could only imitate the white man's creation. Not till after the Civil War was the Negro able to express openly his own musical experience—to reclaim it, as it were—and only then was the way open to the creation of jazz.

In minstrelsy, the American musical theater seemed for the moment to have found its own audience and its own level. The "Ethiopian Opera" was the American answer to the English opera, which really was unsuited to the new country. In England it had appealed to a rising middle class by burlesquing the effete fancies of the nobility in terms of the rabble. In America, neither a nobility nor a rabble offered itself as an apt butt for the humor of popular comedy; the American theater had to find a new target. "Jim Crow" Rice had hit upon the Negro, and the choice was at that time uncannily shrewd, for here indeed was a character everyone in the audience could laugh at, could feel sorry for or superior to, without ridiculing himself or what he himself might have been or might become. Mark Twain recalled how the first minstrel show to play Hannibal, Missouri, perhaps still in the 1840's, burst on the town "as a glad and stunning surprise. . . . Church members did not attend these performances, but all the worldlings flocked to them and were enchanted." And in his own acrid way, he expressed the new, wide American public's reaction to minstrelsy: "It seems to me that to the elevated mind and the sensitive spirit, the hand organ and the nigger show are a standard and a summit to whose rarefied altitude the other forms of musical art may not hope to reach."

AMERICAN TRENDS

A little more than two centuries after the first Englishmen settled in America, a little less than two centuries after the first Africans were brought as slaves, the practice of music had achieved new beginnings in the new land. What had been brought from the Old World and from Africa survived only in greatly altered form. Every older variety of musical practice had been cut back, hybridized, forced to adapt and change, or it had disappeared. By the standards of the European musical practice of which it was supposed to be an offshoot, music in America had not merely failed to advance, it had fallen back. While the Old World had been producing the musical monuments of Bach, Handel, Haydn, Mozart, and Beethoven, the New World had been turning from church music to folk hymnody, from opera to minstrel shows. And the intricate rhythms, the free and spontaneous chant of West African music had been half forgotten and half corrupted by the regular meters and measured melodies of Anglo-Saxon hymns and dance tunes.

But seen in a different perspective, the first two centuries of the New World's music represented not a retreat, but an advance in a new and unexplored direction. Old models had been thrown off and new ones found. From new beginnings—unprepossessing ones, to be sure—a musical culture was assuming forms different from any that had come before. And the enduring concerns that would characterize it were revealed early.

The first concern was to win and hold the public, on whose willingness to pay American musicians would rely for their livelihood. At the same time, there was evident a second concern that would keep the first from leading to mere vulgarization. This was a moral concern to uplift. The singing school signaled deep belief that music was intended to be more than entertainment, that it was intended to edify. Standards of musical value were upheld not only by a few professional musicians from abroad but by American amateurs who believed in the art of music and in the meanest man's capacity for the noble. Music in America would have to find its way with the widest public, but the public would have to be educated to respond to what was finest. If an audience was to be won, it was to be won *upward*.

And so minstrelsy and the singing school established two great complementary trends, one tending to broaden, the other to elevate. The two would persist together as American musical culture grew from these new beginnings, and as it experienced the impact of new waves of influence from the Old World.

Part Two

BUILDING AND SEARCHING

I V

A Question of Taste

The first British and European settlers in America had faced the problem of continuing their musical tradition in an alien environment. If they noted that the American Indians had musical traditions of their own, these were irrelevant to the problem; the Europeans would have sought in vain for any resources in the Indians' music helpful to them in carrying on their familiar musical ways. In this sense, the first encounter of Old World musical practice with the continent of North America had been the meeting of a highly developed musical culture with a land devoid of it.

By the time the end of the Napoleonic Wars set off the first great nineteenth-century waves of immigration into the new United States, the situation was different. The new immigrants found a musical practice begun in America that seemed to stem from exactly the same tradition they had left behind. But the state of it, to their shock, seemed somewhere between primitive and barbaric. Thomas Jefferson's lament over his country's musical shortcomings in Revolutionary days was echoed by newcomers half a century later with a new note of derision. Mrs. Trollope saw barbarism not only in the camp meeting but in the theater as well, where she encountered men without coats and a woman "in the front row of a dress box. . . performing the most maternal office possible." Josef Gungl, who brought a small German orchestra to play light music for the rough Americans, found to his disgust that "circus-riders, rope-dancers, beast-tamers, giants, dwarfs and the like are in such numbers that they may surely be reckoned as forming a certain percentage of the population." Like Mrs. Trollope in the 1830's, Gungl in the 1840's made less money than he had hoped to in the new land of opportunity, and like hers his report (in a German musical journal) was bitter:

The so-called Minstrels have the best business here. . . . They paint their faces black, sing negro songs, dance and jump about as if possessed, change their costumes three or four times each evening, beat each other to the great delight of the art-appreciating public, and thus earn not only well-deserved fame but enormous sums of money.

A pianist from London, Gungl continued, amused the public by singing an American sleighing song accompanied by a string of sleighbells attached to one leg, with an assistant playing an instrument that imitated the cracking of a whip. According to Gungl, this performance pleased the audience so much it had to be repeated before the pianist could get down to the business of the evening—a program including music of Mozart, Bach, Handel, and Mendelssohn, which "not a hand applauded."

Among those widely applauded was Ole Bull, a Norwegian

A Question of Taste

violinist who made a fortune touring the United States in 1843–
44. But he was as much a stunt man as a serious artist. He impressed the initiated by playing on all four strings of his fiddle
at once, and he climaxed his performance, after spinning out a
quiet, plaintive introductory air, by lifting his right foot, "much
in the old-grandfather manner of beating time," and suddenly
bringing it "down with tremendous force on the uncarpeted
stage floor," launching into "The Arkansas Traveler," "the most
reckless, mad, intoxicating jig any dancer ever heard to start the
fever of dancing within him." It was startling, and it won audiences. Henry Russell, an English writer and singer of sentimental
songs who spent nine years in the United States in the 1830's and
so considered himself "half American," later wrote of meeting
Ole Bull in New Orleans. The violinist was disheartened by the
Americans' lack of appreciation of his more serious music. "The
people here prefer the nigger's violin to mine," he told Russell.
The Englishman consoled him, "You must not lose sight of the
fact that, until the beginning of this century, musical culture
was a thing practically unknown outside such towns as New
York, Philadelphia and Boston. . . . The generality of the nation
are young in scientific music." To them "fine music consists of
simple song." Russell knew whereof he spoke. His setting of
George Pope Morris's "Woodman, Spare That Tree" was bringing tears to American eyes wherever he found a stage from
which to sing it.

The early nineteenth century was, indeed, the era of the
minstrels and the sentimental song. The flowery holiday gift
books offered bouquets of songs to the ladies. Publishers brought
out innumerable "songsters," often pocket size and bound in
calf, containing the words and occasionally the music of songs
everyone seemed to love. *The Forget Me Not Songster, The*

American Music

Great Western Songster and Jovial Companion, The New American Singer's Own Book, The Parlor Companion or Polite Song Book, The Museum of Mirth ("the editor having expurgated every line of doubtful propriety"), *The Rough and Ready Songster*, and even *The Temperance Harp*—these and others followed, in content, the pattern of *Elton's Songs and Melodies for the Multitudes*, or *Universal Songster*, which announced itself as "A General Collection of Comic, Negro, Sentimental, Patriotic, Military, Naval, English, Irish, Scotch and American Songs and Ballads; for all Tastes and Occasions. Consisting of the Mirthful, Humorous and Laughter Provoking; the Excentric and Exquisite Ethiopian; Delicate and Beautiful Love Songs; National and Heroic Lyrics;—Hunting Songs and Sea Songs; Duets, Glees and Choruses. Including Several Hundreds of the Most Exquisite Songs, Choisest Melodies and Divinest Harmonies of the World's Minstrelsy."

The minstrels and the sentimental song represented two aspects of the American musical taste of the time. Neither was notable for its sophistication, but both were remarkable for the extent of their prevalence in a country already farflung and diverse. Minstrelsy was the earthier of the two, and at its best, as in the songs of Dan Emmett, its music was a genuine and original expression of expanding America. "Ol' Dan Tucker" and "De Boatman's Dance" were frontier songs made general public property, and "Dixie," most enduring of the dozens of "walk-arounds" Emmett wrote for Bryant's Minstrels in the 1850's and 1860's, belonged to neither North or South, but to the country.

The minstrel and the sentimental aspects of public taste were not, however, necessarily opposed. Although minstrelsy was not at first considered proper entertainment for ladies, its songs were printed along with the favorite sentimental ballads in the gift

A Question of Taste

books and songsters. Moreover, the two strains met to some extent in the widespread and popular performance of singing families—most notably the Singing Hutchinsons of the 1840's—whose programs included sentimental songs along with folk hymns and often temperance and abolition songs. But the most significant meeting of the two came in the songs of Stephen Foster (1826–64). Unlike Dan Emmett, who wrote, played, sang, and lived minstrelsy, Foster came to what he called "the Ethiopian business" only in the 1850's, after he had made a name for himself as a songwriter in the more respectable popular tradition. But even before he committed himself to writing for Christy's Minstrels, his natural bent had been for "plantation songs" with words in Negro dialect, and to that medium he brought a gift for melody as genuine as it was appropriate. If Emmett's songs embodied what was most memorable of minstrelsy, Foster's embodied what was most memorable of the sentimental tradition of the time. It was no accident that music of the frontier and of the Negro affected the expression of both men, or that their songs above all others journeyed west with the wagon trains.

By the middle of the century a distinctive American popular musical practice prevailed in the new towns of the West as in the old centers of the East. It prevailed not only in theaters, concert halls, and churches (a common site of performances in the rural areas), but in homes as well, where the ever-present songster was now beginning to be aided by the piano.

John Behrent had produced the first American piano in 1775, in Philadelphia. Still, in 1800 it was estimated that there were only fifty pianos in Boston, a city of thirty thousand. In 1823, Jonas Chickering of that city moved beyond the experimental stage of piano-making to serious production. He developed a way of constructing pianos with a full cast iron frame which enabled his instruments to withstand the rough rail, river, and canal trip into the American hinterland; by 1837, when William Knabe began manufacturing pianos in Baltimore, Chickering was exporting to Europe. Other piano-makers established themselves in Philadelphia, Albany, and New York and had built a three-million-dollar industry by mid-century. This was quickly expanded by German piano craftsmen arriving in 1848 and shortly after (among them, the young Steinweg brothers, who were joined by their father to establish the firm of Steinway and Sons in 1853). In 1851, 9,000 pianos were made in the United States; in 1860, the number was 22,000.

Ralph Waldo Emerson was surprised, during a mid-century lecture tour, to hear music of a Beethoven piano sonata issuing from a midwestern farmhouse, but it was the quality of the music, not the presence of the instrument, he found remarkable. For even after pianos ceased being out of the ordinary, Beethoven sonatas continued to be rare in American homes. Popular taste ran to noisy battle pieces, like Kotzwara's "Battle of Prague," to sentimental airs, and to hymns.

American taste plagued foreign musicians who came to perform in the new country. They were confronted with a wide and apparently avid audience. In 1850, when the French piano virtuoso Henri Herz ventured to play in San Francisco, a rough new town of 25,000 at the far side of a wild country, the box office had to be equipped with scales to accommodate those who could pay for their tickets only in gold dust. But the audience had preferences that did not always match what the visitors had to offer. Of the many who came, only a few were huge successes. Among these were Ole Bull, Jenny Lind, and Louis Moreau Gottschalk; and only Jenny Lind managed to triumph

A Question of Taste

while remaining, in the words of John S. Dwight's fastidious music journal, "an artist who makes a conscience of her art." That she was able to do so was less a tribute to the discernment of American audiences in 1850–52—or even to her artistry— than to the shrewd showmanship of her manager, P. T. Barnum. Without such a promoter, the other performers had to become showmen. Ole Bull stomped to the "Arkansas Traveler" and played tricks with his fiddle; Gottschalk, endowed with the flamboyant touch of the professional Romantic, was willing to forgo the classics when his audience wanted to hear him roll favorite patriotic airs into a Lisztian fantasy.

Louis Moreau Gottschalk (1829–69) was born in New Orleans, but he was as much a visitor in his own country as were his fellow virtuosi from Europe. When he was not quite twelve, a prodigy already performing in public, his father sent him to Paris for further study and a career. He remained in Europe more than ten years. On either continent he was an exotic. A teen-aged American piano wizard playing (among other music) his own compositions based on Creole melodies was something to which Paris concertgoers of the 1840's were not accustomed. Before he appeared in New York, Gottschalk was the rage of France and Spain and had spent half his life on the far side of the Atlantic. His sensational debut in Niblo's Garden, New York, in 1853, was a triumph, not for American music, but for a brilliant exponent of the pianistic style then in vogue in Europe. In compositions like "The Bamboula" and "The Banjo," Gottschalk's musical inspiration stemmed from the New Orleans of his birth, much as Chopin's stemmed from Poland. But whereas Chopin was able to elevate the fashionable salon style to the level of great art, Gottschalk remained a colorful musical matinée idol. He was celebrated on both sides of the ocean and in both

Americas, but his music lacked the vitality to survive him or to affect the musical creations of others. Gottschalk was the first American to impress the European music world. Yet on American music he left no impression at all.

In addition to virtuoso violinists, pianists, and singers, opera companies and orchestras sought fortunes in the United States in the first half of the nineteenth century. The only city in the United States enjoying regular seasons of opera under a permanent local management was New Orleans. There John Davis, an immigrant from Santo Domingo, built the Theatre d'Orleans in 1813 and rebuilt it, after a fire in 1817, to be "the grandest playhouse in the country." French plays and ballets also were given in the theater, but its focus was on the grand opera and *opéra comique* of Méhul, Boieldieu, Auber, Hérold, Meyerbeer, Rossini, and Donizetti.

Each winter, neighboring planters would bring their families to New Orleans and the French Opera House was filled every evening with a gay and resplendent society. Three times each week, when the performance ended, a great swinging floor was brought down over the parquet, and there was dancing till dawn. Dueling was still in fashion, so precautions were taken to see that the gentlemen left their weapons in the dressing room before going in to the ball.

The New Orleans opera made itself felt in the rest of the country. In 1827, it sent companies touring to Philadelphia and New York, and in 1829 a company en route from Paris to New Orleans paused to give Boston its first taste of French opera. Traveling to or from New Orleans, performers stopped to sing in Cincinnati and St. Louis, both of which were becoming hinterland music centers thanks to their location in the line of travel.

Northern cities relied on imported opera, whether from New

A Question of Taste

Orleans or from across the Atlantic. English comic opera held the stage into the nineteenth century, but the debut of the Garcia opera troupe in New York in 1825 introduced Italian opera in something like the grand manner, and a new vogue was begun. The Garcias' opening performance of Rossini's *Barber of Seville* was largely a family affair. Leading roles were taken by Manuel Garcia and his son, by his wife and by their gifted seventeen-year-old daughter Maria (later, as Maria Malibran, to become a great prima donna). They were competent performers, and they brought with them an orchestra of some eighteen players that was undoubtedly the best New York had heard. With public enthusiasm and curiosity aroused, the Italian opera was at first a resounding success. After a season or two, however, enthusiasm waned. From that time, opera companies, visiting or resident, were to struggle for existence in a country where the form never became quite naturalized.

In these early days, the opera had to fight both the prevailing public taste for native musical entertainments and the persisting frowns of "respectable folk" on theatrical entertainment in general. *Uncle Tom's Cabin* reflected popular preference for native music in one telling bit of dialogue:

St. Clare: . . . But where has my little Eva been?
Eva: Oh! I've been up in Tom's room, hearing him sing. . . . He sings such beautiful things about the new Jerusalem, and bright angels, and the land of Canaan.
St. Clare: I dare say; it's better than the opera isn't it?

The feelings of the moralists were reflected by Thomas Hastings, composer of hymns and author of a *Dissertation on Musical Taste*, first published in 1822. He classified operas "where they belong—among other dramatic works" and noted with satisfaction that in America "this species of composition is unknown. It appears among us only as an exotic from other climes, which is a circumstance on the whole not much to be regretted."

Opera troupes from Italy and from England braved both the opposition and the competition. In 1853 the Pellegrini Italian troupe took *La Sonnambula*, *Norma*, and *Ernani* all the way to San Francisco. Before the Civil War the Parodi Italian company opened a new St. Louis theater considered the finest west of New York. "The house formerly went under the name of 'The Varieties,'" reported *Dwight's Journal of Music*, "but from the multifarious uses to which it had been subjected, had lost all caste with the fashionable part of the community." Unfortunately, even with the theater rehabilitated, "the fashionable part of the community" was not enough to sustain performances over a long period of time. In Cincinnati, also a natural stopping place for all the best visiting artists and opera troupes, the entertainments best patronized were the minstrel shows. Sometimes as many as three different minstrel troupes appeared in the city concurrently, all playing before crowded houses.

Nor was it different in New York. In 1854 the new Academy of Music tried offering low-priced opera performances to "cultivate a taste for music" among a broader public, but without success. *Putnam's Monthly* noted that whereas "every attempt to establish an Italian opera here, though originating with the wealthiest and best educated classes, has resulted in bankruptcy, the Ethiopian Opera has flourished like a green bay tree. . . ." The following year the Academy secured the services of no less a personage than Ole Bull as manager. Recognizing the public's feeling for its own music, and hoping perhaps to repeat the success of his "Arkansas Traveler" on an operatic scale, Ole Bull immediately announced a prize of a thousand dollars for an American opera. Before any prize could be awarded, the operatic venture was bankrupt.

A Question of Taste

Visiting orchestras fared no better. They came most often from Germany, spurred partly by political upheavals in Europe around 1848. The Steyermark Orchestra, Gungl's Orchestra, and most notably the Germania Orchestra plied an arduous way from city to city along the seaboard and west to St. Louis, playing music as substantial as Beethoven symphonies along with dance music and novelties calculated to win an unsophisticated audience. After a year, Gungl returned to Germany. The Steyermark group disbanded. The Germanians, by all accounts the most expert as well as the most serious of the lot, managed to stay together till 1854; then they, too, gave it up. Though the visiting orchestras failed financially, their American ventures were ultimately rewarding both for some of the players and for the country. The small ensembles (the Germanians numbered twenty-four) afforded Americans all the way to the Mississippi a first experience of orchestral playing of professional caliber. The Germanians, further, brought American audiences their first acquaintance with works of Beethoven, Schubert, and even Wagner. After the orchestras disbanded, the musicians dispersed from Boston to Baltimore and westward to Chicago, quickly to be absorbed into the growing musical life of their newfound communities. The Germanians' leader, Carl Bergmann, who settled in New York, and their flutist, Carl Zerrahn, who settled in Boston, were only the most famous of those who made lasting contributions to the musical development of the United States. In return, their adopted homeland gave them the livelihood and security they had lacked in Europe.

With all its frustrations, and despite its lack of anything foreigners recognized as musical culture, the United States was clearly a land of opportunity for enterprising musicians from abroad. A German musical journal of 1828 published a report from America in which the writer, amid the usual derogatory remarks about musical activity and accomplishment in New York, offered this significant observation:

Living is not very expensive here. Young musicians, even of mediocre talent, who are scarcely able to make a living in Germany, can do well here, and are sure, if they are saving, to make their fortune. They will be considered artists of the first rank here. But it is necessary to know English in order to teach.

In the next quarter of a century, the push of European instability and the pull of American opportunity brought such an influx of German musical talent that Americans were moved to protest German domination of the country's musical life.

The basis of an American musical culture had been established by this time, even if its qualities eluded newcomers from Europe. Minstrelsy, sentimental songs, folk hymns, and singing families represented the expanding popular aspect of it. More quietly, but just as surely, the singing schools were at work exerting an elevating influence. The schools not only persisted in their original form; they gave rise to a number of significant new developments. It was, in fact, not the absence of musical culture, but the existence of it—and specifically this more serious aspect of it—that enabled musical immigrants so quickly, easily, and fruitfully to make themselves at home in early nineteenth-century America.

MUSICAL CLUBS: SOWING THE SEED

The singing schools traveled west with the settlers. Wherever a few cabins gathered together in the beginnings of a town, a church and school would appear, soon to be followed by a Yankee singing master complete with songbooks and pitch pipe, ready to impart the secrets of reading musical notes and singing hymns. First in someone's cabin, then in the church or the new

A Question of Taste

schoolhouse or court house or tavern, the singing teacher collected a modest measure of corn or coin for enabling young men and women to share by candlelight the unsophisticated pleasure of harmonizing in "Old Hundred," "Indian Converts," "Romish Lady," or "Captain Kidd." The line between religious and secular music was tenuous. The singing schools were a form of entertainment in territory where entertainments were few and homespun, and the tune books commonly contained secular glees and patriotic songs along with hymns and anthems and fuguing tunes. It was an easy step from the singing school, which emphasized improving music in the church, to musical clubs, which emphasized improving leisure hours.

Such clubs were common in New England before the end of the eighteenth century, and a spirit of competition even grew up among them. A singing school started by William Billings in Stoughton, Massachusetts, in 1774, developed in the next dozen years into the Stoughton Musical Society, which was still active in the twentieth century. When the singing club at Dorchester challenged Stoughton to a contest in 1790, Stoughton won decisively by singing the "Hallelujah" from *Messiah* from memory.

The clubs moved west in the wake of the singing masters. A. W. Thayer found no music "worthy of the name classical" to report from a westward journey in 1852. But he did find "the singing teacher . . . abroad" in the land; "and in some of the larger places, Cincinnati, Chicago, Milwaukee, Cleveland, etc.," he found evidence that "the seed" of musical improvement was "sown." Before the Civil War the step from singing school to choral society had been taken in all those cities and even in San Francisco.

Of the early sowing in Boston, the Handel and Haydn Society

was the first fruit. This society's growth anticipated the pattern of growth of similar organizations soon to be formed in other cities. On one hand, there were choral forces that stemmed from the singing school and the musical society; on the other, instrumental forces that stemmed from the rising influence of musical immigrants and touring virtuosi and orchestras acquainting Americans with orchestral possibilities. The Handel and Haydn Society put itself squarely in the singing school tradition when it announced its "purpose of extending knowledge and improving the style of performance of church music." But its second impetus derived from a German musician, Gottlieb Graupner, who had reversed the usual direction of travel by coming from Charleston to Boston in 1798.

Graupner was an instrumentalist, not a singing teacher; he had been an oboist in Haydn's orchestra in London in 1790–91, and in Boston he organized about 1810 a "Philo-Harmonic Society" in which "musicians from scattered sources"—meaning, no doubt, amateurs as well as professionals—met to play Haydn symphonies for their own pleasure. This orchestra of sixteen seems to have been the first organized in the United States; figuring in the development not only of the Handel and Haydn Society but ultimately also of the Boston Symphony, it earned Graupner the title of "father of orchestral music in America." In 1815, to mark the signing of the Treaty of Ghent, all Boston's choral and orchestral resources were marshaled for a Peace Jubilee concert. The success of the performance led directly to the organization of the Handel and Haydn Society the following year, with Graupner as one of its founders.

The Handel and Haydn Society became a leading element in Boston's musical life and a stimulus to similar organizations soon to appear in other cities. Boston's early musical journal, *The*

A Question of Taste

Euterpeiad, noted with wonder the extent of this kind of activity evident in performances announced for the single month of May 1821. These included a concert of sacred music by the Beethoven Society of Portland, Maine, a "grand oratorio" at Augusta, Georgia, a concert by the Philadelphia Musical Fund Society, *The Creation* by the Baltimore Harmonic Society, an oratorio at Providence, a concert of sacred music by the New Hampshire Musical Society at Hanover, and an oratorio by the Handel and Haydn Society at Boston.

As instrumental music gained a surer foothold, the performance of oratorios like *Messiah* and *The Creation* furnished the musical societies a congenial middle ground between the sacred and the secular. And they were a boon to visiting Italian and British opera singers. When an opera company ran into financial difficulties, the singers were welcomed as soloists in oratorio performances by those who would never have listened to them in the evil theater.

LOWELL MASON: HARMONIZING THE COMMUNITY

At this time, minstrelsy was still embryonic, and though camp meetings were flourishing, their potential as a market for songbooks was not yet suspected. But the singing societies lay close to the earliest note-teaching, songbook-selling propensities of the Yankee singing master. It remained only for someone endowed with the respectable zeal of the old tradition to sense the possibilities for musical mass consumption that the societies represented. The someone was Lowell Mason (1792–1872).

Like William Billings, Mason was an educator and an organizer; he was the Yankee singing teacher with his scope enlarged to an expanding America. He was concerned, as the early singing schools had been, that church music be kept respectable.

American Music

Where William Walker adapted folksongs for rural religious meetings, Lowell Mason looked rather to "proper sources." For many hymns, he adapted tunes from works of Handel, Haydn, Mozart, Beethoven, and Weber. He composed many of his own as well, such as those enduring ones for the hymns "From Greenland's Icy Mountains" and "Nearer My God to Thee." With their dignified cadence and mild, conventional harmonies, Mason's hymns helped establish a vein of American hymnody apart from that of the rugged spiritual songs of the camp meetings and from the zestful fuguing tunes through which so many choirs echoed Billings's enthusiasm.

Mason was born in Medfield, Massachusetts, his American ancestry dating back to the Puritans' landing at Salem in 1630. Though fond of music from childhood, he set out on a career in banking; he left Medfield at twenty to take a position in a Georgia bank. In his spare time he studied music with F. L. Abel (recently from Germany) and led the choir in a Savannah church. Here he assembled his first book of hymns and tried unsuccessfully to have it published. He was almost resigned to failure when he showed it to the organist of the Handel and Haydn Society of Boston, G. K. Jackson. Jackson, organizer of the Peace Jubilee concert that was the Handel and Haydn Society's beginning, recommended that the organization bring out Mason's book under its own imprint. *The Boston Handel and Haydn Society Collection of Church Music* went through twenty-two editions between 1822 and 1858, put the society on a firm financial footing, and established an affinity between Boston and Lowell Mason. In 1827 Mason left Savannah and banking to settle in Boston, where he became music director in three churches and president of the Handel and Haydn Society. But the singing school spirit of reform and improvement was still

A Question of Taste

strong in him, and when an acquaintance returned from Europe alive with the new educational theories of Pestalozzi, Lowell Mason recognized that the key to musical advancement might lie not in training choirs, but in training children.

From then on, Mason's efforts were bent toward the unheard-of goal of bringing music into the curriculum of the public schools, and training teachers to teach it. His success was as remarkable as the goal itself. He arrived step by step. First, he published a song book, *The Juvenile Lyre* (1831), the earliest of its kind, intended not for adults in singing schools but for children in public schools. To protests that only a rare child was musically gifted, Mason answered that even those not greatly gifted could be taught to enjoy both performing and listening to music. Furthermore, he maintained, the study of music would be a moral influence on children from which society itself would benefit. To test his methods and prove his point, he offered free classes for children in the Bowdoin Street Church. (In an Independence Day program in 1831, Mason had a group of children give the first public performance of a patriotic hymn titled "America," written with Mason's encouragement by a divinity student, Samuel Francis Smith, who was unaware that the tune he selected from a German songbook was that of the British national anthem.)

Mason presented the children he was teaching in a series of concerts in 1832 and created a sensation. A year later, he opened an Academy of Music, where again he and a group of associates offered free instruction to Boston children. At the same time, Mason pressed for the introduction of music into the public schools.

Some five hundred children enrolled at the Academy of Music in its first session. As the fame of its achievements spread, the

Academy received a steady flow of requests for advice and information on how music might be made a branch of education in communities as far south as Georgia and as far west as Ohio and Tennessee.

A special committee that had been studying Mason's work reported in 1836 to the Boston school board on the moral, intellectual, and educational value of his program. The committee was convinced that "through vocal music you set in motion a mighty power which silently, but surely, in the end, will harmonize, refine and elevate a whole community." The board was won over, and its failure to appropriate money to pay the teacher whose services it had agreed to engage did not deter Mason. He began teaching music classes in Boston schools without pay. The results were so impressive that money was forthcoming the following year. In 1838, Mason officially became city superintendent of public school music—the first in the United States.

To pursue his goal of training teachers, Mason made use of an institution that had grown directly out of the old singing schools. By the 1830's, it was the practice for singing schools or societies of neighboring towns to come together occasionally in "conventions" to show off their accomplishments and to try performing works beyond the scope of the individual groups. These conventions became a medium for developing teachers as well as choruses. Soon Mason was not alone in his work. Associates like Thomas Hastings, George J. Webb, William Bradbury, and George F. Root helped spread Mason's hope of music for all, especially through the conventions that became widespread in the 1830's and 1840's and the longer "normal institutes" that followed in the 1850's. Out of these institutions came many of the teachers who were to take music into public schools across the country after the Civil War.

A Question of Taste

The conventions had a commercial as well as a musical aspect. They became musical marketplaces where competing songbook publishers, originators of teaching methods, and manufacturers of instruments exhibited, advertised, and sold their wares. The music trades were beginning to sprout, and there were those who feared music as an art might not survive their materialistic influence.

Dwight's Journal of Music sometimes expressed such reservations, but the editor's comment on musical conventions was a clear appraisal of the trend Lowell Mason represented in 1852. Dwight saw the conventions as part of a popular musical movement—"music which begins in singing schools and village choirs, and is for the people." He noted that musicians who held to the classical European tradition were not pleased with the development, with its "cartloads of psalmody of home manufacture, and the Yankee trading shrewdness and seeming charlatanry" of its leaders. To "genuine musicians," this effort to organize "the vulgar, homely taste for music" was musically profane, however orthodox and moral the social roots it stemmed from.

Dwight himself, however, had a deeper insight. To him, it appeared music was "destined to take possession of the American people" in both ways: partly by the natural attraction of fine music, as more and more people came to hear it; and partly through such popular activities as the singing schools and now the conventions, "gradually rising to meet the influence which flows down from the true holy land of Art."

In other words, we think that the Italian opera, the orchestras of trained musicians, who play overtures and symphonies to such as begin to appreciate, the oratorio performances in our cities, the accomplished virtuoso pianists, and violinists, and *cantatrici* who make the tour of our states, give one great impulse to music in this country; and that the teachers classes and conventions, the common-school instructions, the multifarious manuals, psalm books, glee books, etc., of Lowell Mason and his hosts of cooperators and rivals, in this field, do also give another impulse, not to be despised, but showing fruits from year to year, and actually converging towards and promising in due time to meet the first-named influence. That furnishes models, this creates audiences.

JOHN S. DWIGHT: STANDARDS AND MODELS

If Lowell Mason sought to create audiences, John Sullivan Dwight (1813–93) sought to furnish models. The advancement of music in a developing America was the concern of both. Mason sought to further it through potential music-lovers and their capacity for "appreciation"; Dwight sought to further it by asserting standards of excellence, of professionalism, of art. Mason's work over half a century reached millions, of all ages, over the country, and he ended his days wealthy, comfortable, and famous. Dwight reached directly only the subscribers to his journal, never numbering more than about five hundred; he spent his last years in obscurity, after giving up the publication in the belief that "there was no real demand for a high class journal devoted to the interests of music." But as America's first real music critic, and editor of the first important American musical journal, Dwight set a standard of high purpose, seriousness, honesty, and zest which later generations could look up to.

Dwight was born in Boston and studied for the Unitarian ministry at Harvard. A close friend of George Ripley from the 1830's, he was in the inner circle of the Transcendentalists, and later of the Saturday Club, which grew out of Emerson's weekly visits to Boston. (The group included James Russell Lowell, Richard Henry Dana, Longfellow, Harvard's President Eliot, and Charles Francis Adams). An article on music by Dwight

A Question of Taste

appeared in the first issue of the Transcendentalist quarterly, *The Dial* (1840), and he wrote extensively for *The Harbinger* (1845–49), published at Brook Farm, where Dwight lived and taught music and Latin. In 1852, again in Boston, he began a publishing venture of his own, with the moral support of the Harvard Musical Association, of which he was a founder.

Dwight's Journal of Music came out for the first time April 10, 1852, and continued weekly for twenty-six years, fortnightly for three more. Its issues were newspaper-size, usually eight pages. A page or more was given over to advertisements which enrich the journal's picture of the polite musical life of the times with announcements of the latest "Pestalozzian School Song Book," or the first American edition of Beethoven's piano sonatas, or such indispensable home music books as *Piano without a Master, Melodeon without a Master, Guitar without a Master*. In the first issue, Dwight said his motive for publishing such a journal lay "in the fact that Music has made such rapid progress here within the last fifteen, and even the last ten years."

Very confused, crude, heterogeneous is this sudden musical activity in a young and utilitarian people. . . . It needs a faithful, severe, friendly voice to point out steadfastly the models of the True, the *ever* Beautiful, the Divine.

For nearly thirty years Dwight worked at filling that role. His small readership included most of those influential in shaping the musical institutions then developing. Dwight offered reports of the growth of musical activity in every part of the United States, of musical happenings and musical thought in Europe and even in Russia and Japan. Such pioneer American writers on music as Frédéric L. Ritter and W. S. B. Mathews appeared in Dwight's pages; and next to Dwight himself the most regular and frequent contributor was "The Diarist," Alexander Wheelock Thayer, later to write a Beethoven biography that remains a classic in musical literature.

The times called for someone like Dwight and his associates and correspondents to set standards where they were lacking and to encourage those devoted to high goals. Dwight defended the Philharmonic Society of New York, founded in 1842, because in his view it represented the "appreciation" of music not as "a tickling sensation" but as "a genuine delight." Boston's own Musical Fund Society and Mendelssohn Quintette Club, as well as the Handel and Haydn Society, were other youthful institutions to which Dwight offered encouragement and guidance. He watched with considerable anxiety to see how "this most mystical and yet most human Art" of music was faring in the growth of "that most formidable business in our land, music teaching." He had fears about the flood of those "great Yankee staples in trade," the psalm books. The danger was that "they keep creating and keep feeding such a lazy appetite for psalm tunes (which while they seem new never introduce a new musical idea), that really artistic and inspired music is turned away from as something too 'learned' and too 'scientific.' " Still, he considered that Lowell Mason's new New York Normal Institute might benefit American music; the opportunity it afforded teachers to broaden their experience of music "in a musical metropolis" could "even unfold some germs of creative talent."

Dwight came close to grasping the nature of the forces that were coming together in American music. In many ways he was farsighted and progressive; in his pages Americans first read translations of the writings of Richard Wagner and Eduard Hanslick, and he was one of the first to take note of and call attention to Negro spirituals. But while he was able to see a

A Question of Taste

musical movement mounting in the American people, he was unable to embrace it. For he was, in his own thinking, one of those "few alone" who visited "the true holy land of Art." He decried the trend toward Italian and French operatic models and insisted that Beethoven and Mozart posed the only true criteria for aspiring American composers. Preference for these musical models, he said, would be "the very best symptom of our ceasing to be provincial in Art." Provincial he refused to be. "Let the native geniuses wait, as all others had to"; standards could not be lowered to suit them.

PROTEST AND ASPIRATION

The native geniuses were not willing to wait. Furthermore, at least two of them were becoming vocal in their impatience with the European—specifically the German—mold into which they saw American music being forced. Most articulate was William Henry Fry (1813–64), a newspaper editor in Philadelphia. Fry was a musical amateur ardent and industrious enough to have composed an opera, *Leonora*, produced in 1845 by the Seguins' English opera company in Philadelphia. *Leonora* is commonly listed as the first "grand opera" written by an American. For its second production, in New York in 1858, it was fitted out with a libretto in Italian to suit the fashion of the day and the style of Fry's Bellini-like music. In the meantime, Fry had spent half a dozen years in Europe, and had suffered not only a personal but a national affront when *Leonora* was refused for Paris performance. The manager of the opera house told him that as far as Europeans were concerned America was fine for telegraphs and railroads, but that he would be thought crazy if he produced an American opera.

Fry returned to America in 1852 ready to declare the United

American Music

States' musical independence of Europe. He became music critic of the New York *Tribune*—the first music critic of an American daily; and he launched a giant project designed to set the musical score straight. He delivered a series of ten lectures on the whole history and language of music, with a corps of Italian vocalists, full orchestra, chorus, and military band to perform examples. The entire presentation led up to what was on the surface an appeal for the recognition of American composers. More fundamentally, it was a protest against foreign domination. John S. Dwight showed his mettle by reporting Fry's lectures in detail, quoting liberally passages clearly opposed to his own viewpoint. *Dwight's* is the source of the following from Fry's final lecture, a plea for public support for art, mixed with shares of nationalism and nativism:

The only hope for the dramatic future lies in the English or rather American opera. In art, however, as a nation, we need nationality. I am always told that we are new. We are not so new. . . . This city is now twice as large and indefinitely richer than any Italian city was when Haydn and Mozart went there to perfect their art. It has ample wealth to support art properly, but it wants one thing, without which no nation can become artistically great, and that is national spirit. It must encourage art on the spot. It must make a difference between those who come to stay and those who come to go. . . . We allow our chief city to be used as an exchange for every adventurer under Heaven.

Alas, Fry's horizon was as narrow as Dwight's. For him, the true mother of music was Italy, and the real crux of his argument was not so much to advocate American over European models as it was to further Italian over German models.

In his bitterness against the German influence, Fry found a vocal ally in George Frederick Bristow (1825–98). Bristow was a violinist in the Philharmonic Society, conductor of the orches-

A Question of Taste

tra in Fry's lecture series, and composer of overtures, symphonies, and (in 1855) an opera based on Irving's *Rip Van Winkle*. In 1853, both Bristow and Fry were favored by performances of their works by the visiting orchestra (French, not German) of the part-genius, part-charlatan, Louis Antoine Jullien (1812–60). His orchestra, supplemented with New York musicians, was held by some observers to surpass anything that had been heard in America. But it was Jullien's trickery that assured his sensational success. His programs included, for example, a "Fireman's Galop" the climax of which had the ceiling of the music hall burst into flames that were then triumphantly extinguished by a fire brigade. Amid such goings on, the American works Jullien performed were given scant notice in the music journals, a slight from his own countrymen which brought from William Henry Fry a sharp protest in New York's *Musical World and Times*. In his complaint, Fry attacked the Philharmonic Society: it was "an incubus on Art," he wrote, "never having asked for or performed a single American composition during eleven years of its existence."

It was at this point that George F. Bristow entered the fray. As a member of the Philharmonic Society he could attest that the orchestra had indeed given "one whole performance of one whole American overture [and] one whole rehearsal of one whole American symphony." Then in a burst of chauvinism Bristow told the *Musical World*, "As one exception makes a rule stronger, so this single stray fact shows that the Philharmonic Society has been as anti-American as if it had been located in London during the Revolutionary War."

Now in the name of the nine Muses what is the Philharmonic Society in this Country? Is it to play exclusively the works of German masters, especially if they be dead, in order that our critics may translate their ready-made praises from the German? Or is it to stimulate original art on the spot? Is there a Philharmonic Society in Germany for the encouragement solely of American music?

So the nativism of the day expressed itself in the field of music. There was reason, if not justification for it. In 1860, the *Journal of Commerce* counted in New York alone "not far from thirty German societies for the culture of music." These groups met twice a week to practice separately, then came together monthly as a "Saengerbund" to rehearse works requiring many voices. And every year, the New York Saengerbund met with similar bodies in Philadelphia, Baltimore, or Cincinnati, "forming a national organization quite numerous and thoroughly disciplined." Instrumental music was dominated by German players, teachers, and conductors. The Philharmonic Society was for all practical purposes a German orchestra; chamber music in its beginning stage in the United States was under German influence whether in New York, Boston or Milwaukee. How were Americans to make a place for themselves in this German musical world? Where were they to acquire the training and experience to compete with the born and bred disciples of this powerful tradition? Was America to produce only hymns and minstrel songs?

Curiously, the first composer who sought to create an American expression in symphonic terms was a German immigrant, a remarkable character who arrived in the United States in 1810 as Anton Philipp Heinrich and later Americanized his given names to Anthony Philip. Heinrich (1781–1861) began his American life as a musical amateur in Philadelphia, comfortably supported by his family's business in Europe. A succession of tragedies left him without family or fortune but dedicated to a musical career. A violin his sole possession, he traveled on foot

A Question of Taste

from Philadelphia to Pittsburgh, and then on into Kentucky. In a log cabin at Bardstown, Kentucky, he taught himself to compose, hoping deeply that he might be able to express something of his new homeland. When he published his first music in 1820, he said, "No one would ever be more proud than [myself] to be called an American musician."

From his pen came a succession of elaborate tone poems, symphonies, oratorios with titles such as *The Pilgrim Father, Yankee Doodliad, National Memories,* and a "musical autobiography," *The Wildwood Troubador.* In 1837, he settled in New York, where he helped in organizing the Philharmonic Society and came to be called, with love and respect, "Father" Heinrich. When he died—still penniless—he left literally trunks full of his music, some few pieces of which had been performed in testimonial concerts while he was alive. Unfortunately, his gifts were far short of his aspirations. "Father" Heinrich was defeated by the same deficiencies that defeated William H. Fry and George F. Bristow—lack of talent and training.

By 1861, American music was thriving at the popular level and struggling at the level of art. Singing masters from William Billings to William Walker had created an American hymnody suited to the rugged openness of the frontier and the vigor of its people. Minstrelsy had distilled some of the flavor of that frontier and its music into songs and dances unlike any created elsewhere, and Stephen Foster had managed to refine the style without losing its native zest. All these were indigenous expressions, and to master them required no lengthy or intensive technical training. To create in the symphonic or operatic tradition was another matter. Attendance at singing schools or conventions or normal institutes did not begin to approach the preparation needed for it. Children studied singing in the public

American Music

schools, but professional musical training was something the United States had not begun to provide. The time was ripe for it now.

Foreign musicians—those who came to tour as well as those who came to stay—had helped American amateurs to build and educate an American audience. Lowell Mason and his educational effort, John S. Dwight and his insistence on standards of excellence had laid further groundwork. The musical societies were well established, and early efforts to organize orchestras were making perceptible headway. For the first time a young American might realistically entertain the hope of making a profession of serious music. In pursuit of the goal, he would have to equip himself with a kind of training offered only in Europe. In 1842, Gottschalk's going there to study was something out of the ordinary. Two decades later, however, several aspiring American musicians followed him; nearer the end of the century, more and more were to do so.

But in 1861, the country was torn by war.

V

A Rising Nation

When Frédéric Louis Ritter wrote the first historical account of *Music in America* in 1883, he recalled that the outbreak of the Civil War brought the musical life that had been shaping itself in the United States to a momentary standstill. Foreign artists, except for a few opera singers, fled embattled America for Europe. "The only music people cared to hear, people had to hear, was that of the bugle, of the fife, of the drum, calling men to arms."

Both armies had their fighting songs. Confederate troops marched to battle singing "Dixie," captured from the staunchly Unionist Dan Emmett (and drolly reclaimed for the North by President Lincoln when the war ended). The northerners' "Battle Hymn of the Republic" also was borrowed. Julia Ward Howe set its verses to a tune that was first associated with a hymn of uncertain authorship, beginning "Say, Brothers Will You

Meet Us." With its "Glory, Hallelujah!" chorus it had been popular in churches and camp meetings for years before it was appropriated for "John Brown's Body"—in which form, in 1861, it inspired Mrs. Howe to her enduring version.

The war also called forth a number of martial songs, the most memorable being Patrick S. Gilmore's "When Johnny Comes Marching Home" and the rousing "Battle Cry of Freedom" by Lowell Mason's associate, George F. Root. But there were greater numbers of pathetic ballads in the sentimental vein of the popular music of the day. "Lorena," written several years before the war by the Reverend H. D. L. Webster and J. B. Webster, was sung at the campfires of both armies, as were John Hill Hewitt's "All Quiet along the Potomac," George Root's "Just before the Battle, Mother," and Walter Kittredge's "Tenting Tonight on the Old Camp Ground." Musically, the country suffered no division.

Nor was the country's musical development interrupted as Ritter imagined. What he saw as a "momentary standstill" was actually a lull in the direct flow of European influence, a lull like those that had earlier spurred the development of American musical institutions. In music, as in so much of American life, the period around and following the Civil War saw the emergence of new practices that reflected the country's newly accumulated fortunes, its expanding and unifying transportation system, its rising national consciousness. Scattered musical energies that had been expending themselves haphazardly in the first half of the century now came to be focused and consolidated in institutions of American stamp and scope.

The old singing schools were beginning to wane before the war. They were necessarily suspended when the men marched off to battle, and by the end of the war they had become obsolete except in the rural South and frontier West. In the cities the singing school master was supplanted by the public school music teacher, and professional musicians began to establish themselves. George Peabody, a Baltimore merchant and philanthropist, had established a fund for the advancement of the arts as early as 1857; the building of the Peabody Institute, which was to include an academy of music, was begun in 1860. Its completion was delayed eight years by the war, during which time several conservatories had sprung up: the Oberlin Conservatory of Music was founded in Ohio in 1865; the New England Conservatory in Boston, the Cincinnati Conservatory and the Chicago Musical College all began instruction in 1867. The new conservatories were evidence that the profession of music had taken root and would be growing. In 1875, President Charles W. Eliot's Harvard took the step John S. Dwight had long been urging and created the first chair of music in an American university, with John Knowles Paine (1839–1906) as its first holder. Paine, born in Portland, Maine, had been lecturing on music at Harvard since 1862, shortly after he returned from three years' study in Berlin. The year after Paine's appointment as professor, the Music Teachers National Association was organized with Eben Tourjée, founder of the New England Conservatory, as president.

During the war years and in the decade or two following, young American singers like Clara Louise Kellogg, Adelaide Phillips, Annie Louise Cary, Minnie Hauk, Charles R. Adams, and Myron Whitney took places alongside visiting Europeans on the opera and concert stages. Native instrumentalists were rarer; singing lessons had been easier to come by in the United States than competent instrumental instruction, and traditional musical practice continued to be dominated by musicians of

American Music

German origin. The Mendelssohn Quintette Club, for example, was formed in 1849 by members of visiting German orchestras that had disbanded. With Boston as their base, they set out to make chamber music known far from the eastern seaboard, and before the Civil War they had played as far west as Topeka. German musicians in Milwaukee had ventured a season of string quartet music as early as 1850, but this kind of music was generally unknown in the West. Thomas Ryan, who played viola and clarinet in the Mendelssohn Quintette, told how a German settler in an Iowa town helped round up an audience for one of their programs (naturally, consisting mainly of German works) by telling his American friends, "Now you will hear something like music!" At the end of the first piece, his pride was beyond containing and he stood up to shout, "Bully for the Dutch!"

Even in the East, concerts of instrumental music enjoyed no large following. Vocal numbers were customarily inserted into instrumental programs for variety; virtuoso trickery (in the style of Ole Bull or Gottschalk) and an occasional familiar air smoothed the way for the music of Beethoven, Mozart, Schumann, or Mendelssohn. When William Mason (Lowell's son) came home in 1854 from his studies in Germany, instead of establishing himself as America's first resident piano virtuoso, he rebelled against the prevalent spoon-feeding. It seemed to him that his studies with Liszt and his acquaintance with Wagner and the youthful Brahms fitted him for something more serious than improvising simultaneously on "Old Hundred" and "Yankee Doodle" for provincial audiences. Rejecting such a career, he devoted himself to teaching and pioneering in the field of chamber music.

For his first partner, Mason (1829–1908) took the cellist Carl Bergmann, who, having come from Germany as conductor of the Germania Orchestra, had remained in New York to be conductor of the Philharmonic Society. But Mason soon was joined by a rising young violinist named Theodore Thomas, who did not yet suspect that a career as conductor lay ahead of him. Mason and Thomas shared high standards and a sense of mission. By standing on the street and passing out handbills to advertise their concerts, they gradually won an audience in New York City and up the coast. They refused to resort to tricks of showmanship to lure listeners, and though at first they did leaven their programs with occasional vocal numbers, they managed little by little to limit their programs to substantial works of chamber music. The thirteen-year career of the Mason-Thomas Quartette established a standard of chamber music performance and program-making where scarcely any had existed. Before the century closed, Thomas was to perform the same mission for the American symphony orchestra.

Musicians and musical amateurs had often joined together to form symphonic ensembles in American cities in the half-century before the Civil War. Gottlieb Graupner's early orchestral attempts in Boston had been succeeded by a Philharmonic Orchestra under the leadership of the Germania Orchestra's flutist, Carl Zerrahn; and when the Philharmonic failed to survive the war, Zerrahn continued to give concerts under the aegis of the Harvard Musical Association. In New York, the Philharmonic Society was formed in 1842 under the leadership of a German-trained native of Connecticut, Ureli Corelli Hill. It was very distant from the Philharmonic-Symphony of a century later. Essentially a club, it was organized on a cooperative basis, with only the conductor and the librarian receiving salaries. The sixty-odd members, almost all of German background or training, received equal shares of the income from their concerts.

American Music

Fortunately, all relied on other occupations for their living. They played three concerts a year at first, and worked gradually up to eight yearly by the end of the century. In their nadir season of 1876–77, each player netted eighteen dollars! Yet the Philharmonic Society was America's closest approach to a regular symphony orchestra in the mid-nineteenth century. The transition to the symphonic organizations of the present took place in the last quarter of the century. And central in the development was the dauntless, finally triumphant figure of Theodore Thomas (1835–1905).

THEODORE THOMAS AND AMERICAN ORCHESTRAS

Thomas came to America with his family as a boy of ten. His father had been a town musician in the East Frisian (North German) village of Esens. That the son was able to help his father support the family in their new home by playing both horn and violin was a tribute to his musical gifts rather than to any schooling he might have had. He gained his education playing in New York theaters, where he formed a lifelong attachment to Shakespeare and came to know the works of Goethe, Schiller, and Lessing. His musical development was the result of stern self-discipline and of experience ranging from solo appearances (in which he was billed as "Master Thomas," sometimes with the qualification "probably the most extraordinary violinist in the world of his age") to the ballroom ensembles of the Dodworth family, to the orchestra of the Italian opera at the Academy of Music.

Before he was fourteen, Thomas ventured on a tour of the South—alone, often on horseback, carrying a sheaf of posters to advertise concerts by "Master T. T." As he wrote of it later in his autobiography, the trip had a quality of boyish adventure about it. But the experience taught him much about America and its audiences, about his violin, and about his own capacities. He returned to New York resolved to go to Europe for the formal training he lacked, but he found that while he had been away, Europe had come to the United States. German orchestras could be heard, and opera companies were competing for public attention. In New York Thomas could find men to help him in the technical studies of harmony and counterpoint. Supporting himself with a variety of engagements in theaters, in concerts, and at the opera, he put himself through an intensive discipline of study and practice. He heard the visiting virtuosi and learned from them. He listened to Henriette Sontag and Jenny Lind and tried to model his playing after their singing. In 1853, he was one of the New York musicians recruited to fill out the visiting orchestra of the sensational French conductor, Louis Antoine Jullien. For the first time the young violinist heard a full symphony orchestra, and it impressed him deeply, despite his disgust with Jullien's sham and claptrap. The next year he was elected to membership in the Philharmonic Society. The year after that, he began playing chamber music with William Mason. And so he accomplished his musical education, with himself as the principal teacher.

Before he was twenty he had begun to gain recognition as a soloist, but his gift for leadership had begun to assert itself too. He became concertmaster of the opera orchestra and was by common consent leader of the Mason-Thomas Quartette. On December 7, 1860, he stepped in as a last-minute substitute for the conductor at the Academy of Music. He had never conducted an opera before, and the score at hand was unfamiliar to him; but he conducted, and he saved the show. When the management offered him an engagement as regular conductor, he accepted half reluctantly; he did not want his duties to take too much time from his studies. Yet the role attracted him. In fact, the sense of a new purpose was growing in him. Opera conducting did not satisfy him; nor did the role of violinist; nor, in the long run, did chamber music, though he regarded the Mason-Thomas programs as a "cornerstone of American music."

He had played dance music, theater music, opera, chamber music, concerts, recitals—but the symphony, which was for him the richest and loftiest of musical experiences, was what he had in mind when he wrote in his autobiography, "In 1862, I concluded to devote my energies to the cultivation of the public taste for instrumental music." He knew America, and he felt certain it was to be a musical country. What it needed, above all, was "a good orchestra, and plenty of concerts within reach of the people." He put it simply: "I thought the time had come to form an orchestra for concert purposes."

He meant an orchestra of a kind then unknown in America— a professional orchestra, a *permanent* orchestra, securely endowed and dedicated to the edification of the public and the advancement of musical art. He felt certain that if he were to organize such an orchestra, train it, and show what sort of musical experience it could provide, someone would soon come forward from those incredibly prosperous men he saw in the opera audiences to offer the support needed to make the orchestra a lasting public institution. It was an inspired idea, and Thomas miscalculated in only one grave detail: the time had not yet come, it was to arrive through him.

His first concert, in 1862, was the beginning of a thirty-year struggle during which he created in the Theodore Thomas Orchestra an ensemble that observers from abroad ranked above the best that Europe had to offer. He won and educated a new

A Rising Nation

musical public, not only in New York but along a "musical highway" that took him and his orchestra, beginning in 1869, for twenty-one years, from New York to Boston, from Boston west to Chicago and St. Louis, and back through Indianapolis, Louisville, Cincinnati, Philadelphia, Washington, with excursions from time to time through the South, up into the Northwest and Canada, or all the way to San Francisco and back through Texas. Twelve years after his first concert, Thomas was able to say,

Throughout my life my aim has been to make good music popular, and it now appears that I have only done the public justice in believing, and acting constantly on the belief, that the people would enjoy and support the best in art when continually set before them in a clear and intelligent manner.

Yet the hoped-for sponsor did not appear. Thomas was able to keep his orchestra together only by undertaking a brutal schedule of touring in winters and a full calendar of concerts outdoors in New York City parks in summers. He bore not only the physical strain but the financial responsibility for all of it, and despite the orchestra's fame and popularity he was often on the brink of ruin. More than once he went over the edge. A series of Chicago concerts by the Thomas Orchestra was one of the casualties of the great fire of 1871; Thomas went deeply in debt to pay his men for the concerts they were unable to play. Five years later, an ill-advised series of evening concerts during the Philadelphia Centennial Exposition was so costly a failure that Thomas was on the verge of declaring bankruptcy. When the moment of decision came, he could not bring himself to take what seemed to him a weak course; instead he spent the next years laboring to pay his debts in full.

While the firm support he sought for his own orchestra failed to materialize, one new musical institution after another was established in the wake of Thomas's efforts and through his inspiration. In 1873, he created the Cincinnati May Festivals that continued as a distinguished biennial musical event into the present century. In 1877 he was elected conductor of the Philharmonic Society, and during the next fourteen years (with a brief interruption in 1878 when he went to Cincinnati to head a new conservatory) he brought that orchestra for the first time to a professional level of discipline and imbued it with fresh spirit, enabling it to win new prestige and attract capacity audiences. All the while he continued with the Thomas Orchestra and conducted the Brooklyn Philharmonic Society as well! Orchestras in Cincinnati, St. Louis, Philadelphia felt Thomas's influence both directly and through the force of his orchestra's example. And in Boston he helped bring into being America's first endowed symphony orchestra. When he took the Thomas Orchestra there in its first tour, in 1869, *Dwight's Journal* served notice to the local musicians: "We shall demand more of our own in the future. They cannot witness this example without a newly kindled desire, followed by an effort to do likewise." Annually for a dozen years Thomas returned to Boston to renew the inspiration, and at last, in 1881, the Boston Symphony Orchestra was founded to satisfy the appetite he had aroused. It was established by the personal endowment of Henry L. Higginson, a musically inclined financier of the kind Thomas had imagined must one day come forward in symphonic music's behalf. As Major Higginson himself said, "Theodore Thomas made the Boston Symphony Orchestra possible." But a German musician, Georg Henschel, was imported to be its first conductor.

For Thomas, the 1880's brought popularity and then despair.

A Rising Nation

While his dream of a permanent orchestra remained unfulfilled, he became involved in a grand but fatally mismanaged venture called the American Opera Company, which brought him again to financial ruin. His prestige suffered, and he found his concert audiences dwindling. Tragedy followed tragedy. In 1888, his financial situation forced him to disband his orchestra. The next spring, Mrs. Thomas died. It was small consolation to Thomas that friends across the country arranged a "triumphal march" of command performances of the Thomas Orchestra (reassembled for the occasion) in twenty-five cities. He now saw himself, at fifty-three, alone, at the end of a career that seemed to have failed in its whole purpose.

It was not, however, the end. At the low point of his life—his wife mortally ill, his orchestra disbanded—Thomas was approached by a Chicago businessman, Charles Norman Fay, with a proposal that he come to Chicago to establish an orchestra. Fay was prepared to form a board of Chicagoans to contribute the money necessary to maintain the kind of orchestra Thomas had dreamed of. Would he come? Thomas's reply flashed with his unquenchable determination: "I would go to hell if they would give me a permanent orchestra."

Thomas's years in Chicago, from 1891 till his death in 1905, were by no means free of reverses, but they bore lasting fruit in the form of the Chicago Symphony Orchestra and its home, Orchestra Hall. Thomas was not satisfied simply to have his "permanent orchestra"; he wanted it permanently housed in a hall more suitable for concerts than Louis Sullivan's great auditorium. The members of the board were persuaded, and they brought their own vision to bear on the plan. The new hall would not only be a home for the orchestra; it would contribute to the orchestra's support by earning rent. Further, it would be built in part through contributions of the wealthy, but in part by general public subscription. So it was, with eight thousand contributors sending from 10¢ to $25,000. Theodore Thomas conducted the inaugural concert in Orchestra Hall, December 14, 1904. He died of pneumonia a few weeks later. But he had lived to set the pattern of the modern American symphony orchestra, not only in its standard of performance, the range of its programs, and the make-up of its audience, but also in its means of support, by voluntary contributions not merely of a few wealthy patrons but of the musical public.

The pattern did not take hold immediately. Professional symphony orchestras were established before 1900 in St. Louis, Pittsburgh, Cincinnati, and Los Angeles, as well as in New York, Boston, and Chicago, but until well into the present century they were sustained by the generosity of a few who had accumulated fortunes in the country's business and industrial expansion. Walter Damrosch (1862–1950) succeeded in mobilizing the Carnegies, Rockefellers, Vanderbilts, and Morgans to support the New York Symphony which his father Leopold (1832–85) had founded in 1878 to compete with the Philharmonic Society. In other cities, other wealthy men—Ryerson, McCormick, Armour (and others) in Chicago, Brookings in St. Louis, Clark in Los Angeles, Bok in Philadelphia, Taft in Cincinnati, Pulitzer in New York—subsidized or endowed symphony orchestras. Like Boston's Major Higginson, these men thought it appropriate

in a Republic that the citizens and not the Government in any form should do such work and bear such burdens. To the more fortunate people of our land belongs the privilege of providing the higher branches of education and art.

For men who shared Higginson's view, music was no frivolous diversion; it had to do, as the Puritans would have had it, with

A Rising Nation

the nourishment of the mind and spirit. To foster it was to foster morality. To propagate music among the people was to lift them up spiritually, and "uplift" was a theme of the times. Nor was anyone more conscious of an educational mission than Theodore Thomas. In his Central Park Garden concerts, beginning in the 1860's, he recalled the purpose of the early singing school teachers by deliberately shaping his programs to introduce the light-music-loving public to more and more serious and substantial music. In 1883–84, he played what seems to have been the first series of concerts designed for audiences of children. Before the end of the century, the Boston Symphony was playing children's concerts regularly, as were the Damrosches, Walter and Frank, in New York.

A NEW OPERA HOUSE

While symphony orchestras were multiplying, and were both discovering and cultivating an audience, opera struggled to establish itself in America without comparable success. For latter-day Puritans, it still bore the stigma of Theater (according to Ritter, "clergymen warned their congregation against patronizing an entertainment which they considered immoral and full of worldly temptations"). And for a theatergoing public used to minstrel shows and *Uncle Tom's Cabin*, opera's pomp and artifice, not to mention the language, seemed largely alien. Its appeal was connected less with music than with social prestige; indeed, among its patrons were enough prosperous men of industry and finance that in 1861 the newly elected president took the trouble to put in an appearance at the Academy of Music as he passed through New York en route to Washington. Arriving after the overture (the opera was *Ballo in Maschera*), he entered the dress circle so quietly that the first act was over before the audience realized who was there. Then they rose and gave him an ovation. The *Herald* reporter left no doubt that the westerner with the incipient whiskers (and doubtful black gloves) had come among the elite:

It may well be considered one of the most flattering ovations yet offered Mr. Lincoln in the Empire State, and coming as it did from a class of citizens whom the President-elect could not have had so excellent an opportunity of seeing assembled together under any other circumstances—and in consideration of the wealth, intelligence and respectability of those who were so met together—the demonstration becomes doubly valuable and will not, as it should not, be readily forgotten by Mr. Lincoln.

After the war, new wealth sought the pleasures of the old, but the "Knickerbocker gentry" held stiffly to their boxes at the Academy of Music, disdaining to admit newcomers to the inner circle of the opera's patrons. There was nothing for the newcomers to do but to build themselves a new opera house; and so in 1883 the Metropolitan Opera arose, with seventy boxes to the Academy's thirty. There, Vanderbilts and Morgans, Jay Gould, William Rockefeller, James Harriman, and their peers reigned as Henry E. Abbey produced a season of Italian opera that was lavish but disastrous. It ended with a rumored loss of $600,000. The field was not, however, to be abandoned to the aristocrats of the Academy. The Metropolitan's founders struck out in a new direction, following a suggestion of Dr. Leopold Damrosch, who offered to mount a season of German opera using the Symphony Society as the orchestra. The scheme worked, and after Damrosch died in 1885, it continued to work—even to improve—under Anton Seidl. One more year of costly competition, and James Henry Mapleson, who was producing the Italian opera at the Academy of Music, capitulated with a final taunt: "I cannot fight Wall Street."

The Academy was not alone in feeling the effects of Mapleson's departure. For eight years, the British impresario had been responsible for organizing companies that furnished the major opera performances in American cities, as many as 167 performances in a season. Beginning in 1878, Mapleson produced not only two months of opera in the winter and another month in spring in New York, but also a two-week season in Boston and a week in Chicago, Cincinnati, St. Louis, Philadelphia, Washington, and Baltimore. His repertoire included familiar works of Rossini, Donizetti, Bellini, Meyerbeer, and also newer operas by Verdi and Wagner (*Lohengrin* in Italian), Gounod's *Faust*, and in 1878 the first American performance of *Carmen* (also in Italian). His casts included, along with leading European singers, American prima donnas—Clara Louise Kellogg, Annie Louise Cary, Lillian Nordica, Minnie Hauk, Alwina Valleria (who in 1883 became the first American to sing at the Metropolitan), and the Emmas Abbott, Juch, and Nevada.

Having secured the field in New York, the Metropolitan, with German casts, presented the first American performances of Wagner's *Das Rheingold*, *Siegfried*, *Götterdämmerung*, *Die Meistersinger*, and *Tristan und Isolde*. Opera belonged to the fashionable, however, and the fashion for Wagner began to pass. The Metropolitan switched from the German back to Italian and French operas, survived a fire in 1892, changed managers, and toward the end of the century entered its "Golden Age of Song." Through it all, at the Metropolitan as at Chicago's Auditorium (which a company under Henry Abbey's management inaugurated in 1889), opera was a tenant rather than a homeowner. The sponsoring social lions provided a house in which they themselves could occupy the boxes, then leased the stage to a manager who produced an opera season as a commercial enterprise. Expected not to lose money, he hoped to make a profit—

and, at least in the case of the Metropolitan's Maurice Grau, he sometimes did. Smaller ventures were not always so fortunate. Troupes formed, traveled, ran into difficulties, and dissolved with seeming unconcern, re-forming, traveling, and dissolving again. A few, including the companies headed by Clara Louise Kellogg and Emma Abbott (which presented opera in English) managed to survive for a number of years, and brought a taste of opera to audiences in many parts of the country.

Between American and European opera engagements, leading singers often joined "concert parties" that traveled widely and profitably in the last quarter of the century in programs of instrumental and vocal solos, chamber music, and favorite opera excerpts. It was not unusual for a group of half a dozen artists to tour together for a month, making their way from Milwaukee to Duluth, Dubuque, Des Moines, Kansas City, St. Joseph, Atchison, and back to Cincinnati.

The musical public was expanding, as was the profession, and together they now called into being new musical journals and the beginnings of an American literature about music. *How to Understand Music*, published in 1880 by W. S. B. Mathews (1837–1912), was an early entry in the growing list of books aimed at initiating the "layman" into the supposed secrets of concert music. Mathews was one of John S. Dwight's correspondents, an organist and singing teacher in the old tradition. He later (1891–1902) published a monthly journal for music teachers, *Music*, and wrote a historical survey of *A Hundred Years of Music in America* (1889). In the latter instances he was early in the field, but not the first: *The Musical Courier* had begun publication in New York in 1880, and *The Etude* first came out in Philadelphia in 1883, both still being read by music teachers half a century later. It was in 1883, too, that Frédéric L. Ritter

A Rising Nation

published *Music in America*, the first comprehensive work on the subject and still valuable despite its biases.

The nation was becoming conscious of itself, musically as otherwise, and there was a rising tendency to undertake musical ventures of national scope. As the singing schools faded, the yearly conventions they had given rise to developed in a direction of their own: they became the basis of festivals modeled after those of England and the European continent. Shedding their original pedagogical purpose, they now occasioned massed performances of major choral works of Handel, Haydn, Mozart, and Beethoven. Carl Zerrahn had ventured such an affair under the auspices of Boston's Handel and Haydn Society in 1857; in 1868 the Handel and Haydn Society Festival was established as a triennial event. Zerrahn also took over the musical conventions in Worcester, Massachusetts, and by 1866 they had been transformed into an annual festival in which twenty towns and villages participated. In the ensuing three decades festivals sprang up in large cities like Cincinnati and Chicago, in small ones like Ann Arbor, Michigan, and Mt. Vernon, Iowa. Theodore Thomas is said to have conducted as many as a dozen festivals in a season, in different cities with different programs.

The most spectacular mass performances were organized by the composer of "When Johnny Comes Marching Home," Patrick Sarsfield Gilmore (1829–92), in Boston in 1869 and 1872. Ephemeral as they were, Gilmore's Peace Jubilees provide a musical paradigm of the times in the United States. They offered "a type for all"—song, symphony, spectacle, ballyhoo, and respectability to boot. John S. Dwight would have none of them. He warned his readers that Gilmore's "General Committee,"—

listing, among others, Longfellow, Emerson, Holmes, Lowell—
was "a snare and a delusion . . . one of the shrewd advertising
dodges in which the average jubilee brain is so fertile." Indeed,
a Gilmore Jubilee was not for purists; it was for the public, the
market—and it sold. Gilmore was an organizer, at home in an
age of organizers.

Born in Ireland, he came to Massachusetts through Canada,
making his way by playing in militia bands. In 1859, in Boston,
he formed a band of his own, the first in a long succession of
Gilmore's Bands. When the war began, he and his men paraded
the streets of Boston drumming up recruits for the Massachusetts Twenty-fourth Regiment. They were so effective that they
recruited themselves. The entire band volunteered and went to
war with the Twenty-fourth. Serving in North Carolina, Gilmore boosted the soldiers' spirits by organizing regimental
minstrel troupes. Then he was taken to New Orleans to be chief
bandmaster for General Nathaniel Banks. There in 1864 he
produced his first spectacle, a huge music festival for which he
mobilized five thousand school children and all the military
bands within range. Marshaling, organizing, and manipulating
large forces to bring off a grand effect was an experience that
touched something in Gilmore. Back in Boston after the war, he
gave a series of concerts, went into the business of manufacturing band instruments, and waited for the right moment, the right
idea. It came to him in 1868: a Great National Peace Jubilee to
celebrate the country's regained unity.

Gilmore envisioned the Jubilee on an extravagant scale and
set about realizing his vision. A building was erected in Boston
to house an audience of fifty thousand. Musical societies and
choruses from all over New England were mobilized to form a
massed chorus of ten thousand. For the orchestra, musicians were

A Rising Nation

marshaled a thousand strong, with Ole Bull and Carl Rosa sharing the first stand of the violins. A great organ was built for the occasion, and so was a bass drum, the head of which "may have been ten or twenty feet in diameter." All winter, Carl Zerrahn (who was to conduct) and Eben Tourjée (who was in charge of the choral forces) traveled from town to town drilling choruses, rehearsing musicians. Every New England village contributed its quota of choristers; all were supplied with music; and the leader of each group was instructed in the precise tempo of every piece to be performed.

Participants came from as far west as Omaha, and special railway parties brought visitors from faraway California on the transcontinental railway completed just a few weeks before. The enormous Jubilee began June 15, 1869, and lasted five days. Writing about it later, Thomas Ryan recalled that "the musical part—all things considered—was noble and dignified." There was even occasion, in the course of events, for two of America's most respected composers, John Knowles Paine and Dudley Buck (1839–1909), to conduct some of their own music. The tone of the Jubilee, however, was set in the opening program, which offered something for everybody. It began with a hymn, "A Mighty Fortress," and moved by way of the Gloria from a Mozart Mass to opera overtures by Rossini (*William Tell*) and Wagner (*Tannhäuser*); "America," with the audience joining in, provided a fitting patriotic conclusion.

But the climax came in the next-to-last number, the "Anvil Chorus" from *Il Trovatore*. For this, Patrick S. Gilmore himself took the baton. Massed chorus, orchestra, military band, drum corps, and organ were supplemented by a hundred red-shirted firemen who entered smartly in two files, carrying blacksmith's hammers at right-shoulder arms. The singers caroled forth, a hundred hammers struck a hundred anvils; all the chimes of the city joined in and more—cannons, fired to Verdi's measure by Gilmore's touching an electric button at the conductor's stand. The overwhelmed audience recovered sufficiently to demand an encore, and got it. When President Grant attended two days later, with Admiral Farragut and party in full regalia, the Great National Peace Jubilee reached a high tide of success.

When in 1872 he seized on the end of the Franco-Prussian War to mount a World Peace Jubilee, with choral forces doubled, Gilmore failed to match his success of 1869. He brought to Boston famous bands of the British Isles, France, Germany. Johann Strauss, Jr., conducted daily concerts of his own music and paraded through Boston attended by "a valet in gorgeous livery, a cockade in his hat." An American group, however, furnished the second Jubilee's remembered moments. The thirteen singers, who had begun performing publicly only the year before, came from Fisk University—founded in 1866 at Nashville to educate freed slaves. And under George L. White's direction, they sang Negro spirituals for audiences that had never heard such music before. When they appeared in Boston in 1872, their singing of "The Battle Hymn of the Republic" brought the audience of twenty thousand to its feet, waving handkerchiefs and shouting "The Jubilees! The Jubilees forever!" As the Fisk Jubilee Singers, then, they traveled to England and the Continent, as well as in the United States, acquainting audiences with a musical treasure just then beginning to be uncovered.

Gilmore staged one more Jubilee, in Chicago in 1873. Then he settled down to the work that was to be his enduring contribution (besides "When Johnny Comes Marching Home") to the country's musical life. As director of the Twenty-second Regi-

A Rising Nation

ment Band of New York, more familiar simply as Gilmore's Band, he brought the concert band to a level of musical accomplishment it had not known before in the United States. Bands were not new in the country. The U. S. Marine Band had made its debut when John Adams was president, and the tradition of militia bands had been sustained in three wars. After the Civil War, the regimental bands disbanded, but the players did not give up playing. Town bands, fire department bands, lodge bands, trade organization bands, company bands sprang up all across the country. Before 1890, it was estimated that there were more than ten thousand amateur military-type bands in the United States, and there were probably twice that many by the end of the century.

Well into the 1900's, until films, phonograph, radio, and jazz changed musical entertainment entirely, amateur bands were indispensable to the festivities of American communities. The amateur players in turn furnished the nucleus of ready audiences for Patrick S. Gilmore and his successors, men like John Philip Sousa, Alessandro Liberati, Frederick W. Innes, who crisscrossed the country with their professional bands during the decades following Gilmore's death. Their programs consisted of marches, waltzes, popular melodies, soloists' showpieces, and a sprinkling of overtures transcribed from orchestral literature. They aimed to entertain, not to edify, and a remark of Theodore Thomas gives wry testimony to their success. After struggling to provide lofty musical programs for the country's first two World's Fairs, Thomas was asked to suggest a musical plan for the one to take place in St. Louis in 1904. His resigned advice was, "Have plenty of band music, out of doors."

The World's Fairs were another manifestation of the country's rising consciousness of itself as a nation among nations. Both the International Centennial Exposition at Philadelphia in 1876 and the World's Columbian Exposition at Chicago in 1893 included music in a scheme to demonstrate America's prowess in many fields. At Philadelphia, emphasis was more on industrial than on artistic achievement, but nonetheless a concert under Theodore Thomas's direction was considered the appropriate way to inaugurate the festivities. For the occasion, major works for chorus and orchestra were commissioned from those reliables, Paine and Buck—from Paine, a *Centennial Hymn* to words by Whittier, and from Buck, a *Centennial Meditation of Columbia*, for which the poet-musician Sidney Lanier wrote the text. In addition, to give the program not just national but world significance, Thomas persuaded the women's committee of the exposition to commission a "Centennial March" from Richard Wagner. To Thomas's disillusionment, the master honored the New World by producing a blatant piece of fustian, for which he demanded a plump five thousand dollars in advance.

For the Columbian Exposition of 1893, Thomas, as musical director, designed a vast plan of events to demonstrate American musical achievement to the world and at the same time to acquaint Americans with the achievements of other nations. Luckless once more, Thomas was able to realize only part of the impressive schedule before it was cut off by a pincers of petty business rivalry and financial pressure.

The trouble began when Thomas insisted on Ignace Jan Paderewski's right to perform on a Steinway piano even though Steinway was not among the piano manufacturers exhibiting at the fair. The exhibiting piano-makers sought to undermine Thomas's position as director, and the Panic of 1893 tipped the balance. The program was unable to survive both the conflict and the financial situation.

A Rising Nation

Even so, Thomas was able to sustain the plan through three and a half of the projected six months; some two hundred musical programs took place, half of them conducted by Thomas himself. The schedule brought symphony orchestras from New York and Boston, choral societies from two dozen American cities, including the historic one from Stoughton, Massachusetts. There were bands ranging from Sousa's and Gilmore's to ensembles from Iowa, Illinois, and Ohio towns, the Garde Républicaine of France, and the Royal Scottish Pipers. Eminent soloists, European and American, appeared, and leading composers and conductors were invited from abroad.

Along with choral societies, symphony orchestras, and bands, the programs presented music by a list of American composers considerably longer than had been the case at Philadelphia. Paine's name still led it—the inaugural concert began with his new "Columbus March and Hymn"—but younger men were heard from too. George Whitefield Chadwick (1854–1931), the leader of an emerging "Boston school" of composers, set music to a dedicatory ode written by Harriet Monroe for the inaugural concert. Later programs brought works by Edward MacDowell (1861–1908), Arthur Foote (1853–1937), Harry Rowe Shelley (1858–1947), and the expatriate Arthur Bird (1856–1923).

For the opening of the Women's Pavilion, Thomas scheduled a program of music by women composers, including Mrs. H. H. A. Beach (1867–1944) of Boston. And out of the fair came an organization that involved women and music on a national scale. Amateur women's musical clubs from all parts of the country held an assembly at the exposition, with the aim of "showing the world the character of the educational work being accomplished" in music by American women. The eight sessions of the assembly generated a movement to organize the clubs nationally, and before the end of the decade the National Federation of Music Clubs was a reality.

National musical organizations, American ensembles touring cross-country, festivals, jubilees, expositions in which American musicians bid for national attention and international consideration, the first chronicles of the country's musical history—all these signaled that by the last quarter of the century, the art of music was being cultivated in the United States on a national scale.

AN AMERICAN SCHOOL?

Fresh and strong as national consciousness was, it is not surprising that the question arose, as W. S. B. Mathews pondered it in *A Hundred Years of Music in America* (1889), of "the creation here of a school of American music." Indeed, it appeared to some that the country's laboriously built musical apparatus was intended to make more Americans appreciate the kind of music Europeans enjoyed, and to encourage Americans to produce the kind of music Europeans produced. American artists and ensembles had emerged—to perform European works. American composers were showing their mettle—in following European models.

The paradox was strikingly illustrated in two ventures of an extraordinary woman named Jeanette Thurber (1851–1946), who concerned herself energetically, and financially, with the establishment of institutions intended to bear a national stamp: the National Conservatory of Music, founded in 1885, and the American Opera Company (and its equally ephemeral successor, the National Opera Company), which toured the country in 1886 and 1887. Financial disaster did not prevent the traveling

A Rising Nation

companies, under Theodore Thomas's musical direction, from proving that opera could be splendidly produced with casts and chorus almost wholly American. But they performed *only* European works in English translation. There was irony, too, in the story of the National Conservatory. In establishing it, Mrs. Thurber obtained a charter not only from the state of New York but also from the Congress of the United States—the earliest instance of national legislation on music. Yet the conservatory's first director was a Belgian opera singer, and when in 1892 the chair went to a celebrated nationalistic composer, he was a Bohemian nationalist, Antonin Dvorak.

Dvorak was dismayed to find that the musical folklorism flourishing in Europe for a full generation was hardly to be found in the United States. Well before mid-nineteenth century, composers in Europe and Russia had begun to exploit folk music in serious works, and by the 1860's musical nationalism was on the rise, not least as a form of rebellion against the prevalence of German musical models in non-German countries. "The Five" (Mili Balakirev, César Cui, Modest Mussorgsky, Alexander Borodin, and Nikolai Rimsky-Korsakov) in St. Petersburg, Tchaikovsky in Moscow, Smetana in Prague, Grieg in Norway, and Dvorak himself had brought the national movement in music to a peak years before Dvorak came to New York.

It took the Bohemian visitor only a short time to become aware that there were indigenous musical materials available to the American composer no less than to the European. Within a few weeks after his arrival in New York, he set to work on a symphony "From the New World," consciously allowing its melodies to be affected by the American plantation songs that appealed to him so strongly as they were sung for him by one of his pupils, a Negro, Henry Thacker Burleigh (1866–1949).

American Music

During his three years in America, Dvorak encouraged those who studied with him to use whatever native materials they could discover, in order to create a national music for the United States. The plantation songs, whether authentic Negro creations or inventions of Stephen Foster, were to Dvorak "the most striking and appealing melodies that have yet been found on this side of the water." But he did not urge these as the only source of "inspiration for truly national music." As he wrote in a farewell article in *Harper's* (not *Century*, as sometimes cited) in February 1895, "It matters little whether the inspiration for the coming folksong of America is derived from the negro melodies, the songs of the Creoles, the red man's chant or the plaintive ditties of the homesick German or Norwegian. Undoubtedly the germs for the best of music lie hidden among all the races that are commingled in this great country." One day, he predicted, a genius would emerge "who will be as thoroughly representative of his country as Wagner and Weber are of Germany, or Chopin of Poland."

Arthur Farwell (1872–1952) founded the Wa-Wan Press in 1901, explicitly to accept "Dvorak's challenge to go after our folk music." He bent his full effort toward gaining recognition for American composers who valued their individuality above European tradition, and a good part of the music published by Wa-Wan between 1901 and 1911 looked (like Farwell's own) to folk music for material and inspiration. Closely associated with Farwell in the publishing venture was the gifted Henry F. B. Gilbert (1868–1928), whose later *Comedy Overture on Negro Themes* and *Dance in the Place Congo* are among the sturdiest products of American musical folklorism. Among thirty-five other composers in the Wa-Wan catalogue were two pupils of

A Rising Nation

Dvorak, Harvey W. Loomis (1865–1930) and Rubin Goldmark (1872–1936), who later was to teach George Gershwin.

None of the music of the Wa-Wan Press has remained current, but in the scores he published and in his prefaces to the publications, Farwell entered a spirited bid for freshness among composers and receptivity among the public. The appeal was delivered in a tone more constructive and confident than that of the tirades of Fry and Bristow half a century before. Farwell may have overstated the case when he said Wa-Wan was "an outcome of the rapid growth of true musical genius in America." Yet the new generation of composers was able to build on a foundation of a sort Fry and Bristow, for example, had altogether lacked.

The most accomplished and celebrated among that generation, Edward MacDowell, rejected Dvorak's thesis. In his lectures at Columbia University, he voiced the hope of hearing American music echo not folklore but "the youthful optimistic vitality and undaunted tenacity of spirit that characterizes the American man."

There was nothing definably American about MacDowell's music, even when he made use of Indian melodies; but he wrote with a technical fluency and a spark of individual sensibility that set his work above the respectable solemnities of Paine or Buck, not to mention the unformed attempts of Bristow, Fry, or Heinrich. The music of the best of MacDowell's contemporaries —Chadwick, Foote, Horatio Parker (1863–1919)—was on a level with his own. Together with several of only slightly lesser talent, they constituted the first generation of soundly trained, professional American composers to work in a context of established musical institutions reasonably receptive to their efforts.

American Music

The emergence of an American national musical style continued to concern certain composers and American writers on music in the early decades of the twentieth century. For some it was a simple matter of national pride, but for others the concern went deeper. Lacking a musical vernacular, the American composer might be unable to reach the broad public that should be his.

V I

Shaping New Forms

For better or worse, by the end of the nineteenth century the descendants of the country's early settlers had succeeded in doing, as Americans, what their forebears had been unable to do as Englishmen and Europeans. They had transplanted the Old World's musical culture to the New. Anglo-European musical practice had been brought to America, had encountered a merciless wilderness, had struggled, suffered a number of indignities, and yet endured.

Less clear was the outcome of that other encounter, the meeting of the Anglo-European with the musical heritage of the Negro slaves in the American South. The development of institutions for carrying on European musical practice in the United States took place in a fairly direct progression, paralleling the development of American society itself. The Civil War came, in the course of this, less as an interruption than as a violent meshing of gears that enabled the development to continue in the same direction at a new pace and on a new scale.

In contrast, the war destroyed once and for all the social structure that had given rise to the music in which the Negro played a part. If that music was to develop further, it would have to be on a wholly new basis. When the historic volume of *Negro Slave Songs of the United States* (by Lucy McKim Garrison, William Francis Allen, and Charles P. Ware) was published in 1867, it uncovered for the world a music that was already of the past. The Fisk Jubilee Singers, introducing Negro spirituals to enthralled audiences in 1871, were singing a classical repertoire of songs which had risen out of the historical experience of a people in an era ended by war. Spirituals endured because their beauty and the depth of religious feeling they embodied were imperishable. But after Emancipation, the musical creativity of the Negro American found new forms of expression.

To begin with, he reclaimed the music expropriated by white Americans when they concocted minstrelsy. A few Negroes had performed on the minstrel stage before the war; after the war, Negro troupes of minstrels multiplied and prospered. At first the Negro performers actually blacked and painted their faces in imitation of the stereotype established by the white minstrels. But with Emancipation, blackface minstrelsy lost whatever validity it might have had. It hung on, and even thrived into the 1890's, but by that time real Negroes had stopped imitating a white entertainer's caricature of imaginary Negroes. The stereotype had lost its charm for all but the simplest rural audiences.

Postwar minstrelsy did produce at least one song of a durability close to that of the prewar music of Foster and Emmett, "Carry Me Back to Ole Virginny," written in 1878 by James

Bland (1854–1911). An early graduate of Howard University, Bland tried unsuccessfully to find work in white minstrel troupes, then joined Billy Kersands's Negro company and later toured in Europe and England with the topnotch Callender-Haverly Minstrels. Another of his songs, "Oh Dem Golden Slippers," was a good example of the postwar Negro minstrel's effort to furnish the white public with music to fit the notion of "Negro music" that had been popularized by minstrelsy.

The time had come for the Negro's music, as it had been recreated in minstrelsy, to take new nourishment from its own roots—from Negro musical practice in the South and West. The way back was complicated by the fact that Negro musical practice was changing with the Negro's place in American life. What took place was not a return—there was no returning—but new mixings and meetings which culminated, as the century turned, in the music called jazz.

The banjo tunes of plantation Negro musicians had been a principal source of the music white musicians created for minstrelsy before the Civil War. Minstrelsy had captured some of the flavor and syncopation of the banjo players, and white audiences everywhere had been charmed by the music. They had come to know, too, the minstrel version of the Negroes' strutting "cakewalk." In the decades following the war, the banjo-players' musical style and the cakewalk's strutting rhythm were fused in a new kind of piano music called "ragtime."

Ragtime was not plantation music, nor even folk music. It was a style of syncopated performing in which the rhythm of the cakewalk (which in the postwar minstrel show came to take the place of the "walk-around" finale) was set off by tricky off-beat manipulations that echoed the banjo accompaniments to minstrelsy's popular "coon songs." As Negro performers found places in the entertainment field after the war, they infused the blackface minstrels' banjo music with zest of their own. And as more Negro musicians began to take up European musical instruments, some began transferring the music from the minstrel band to the piano. No one can say exactly when ragtime piano-playing began, but it probably had been underway for a decade or more before the first pieces of music titled "rags" were published in the 1890's.

Ragtime piano's saucy syncopation fascinated the white patrons of the honky-tonks of the midwestern (not southern) Mississippi riverfront where it seems to have originated. And because a good number of the men who played it were schooled musicians, they began to write the music down for others to play. Ragtime was respectably far from anything really primitive, but it was informed by a rhythmic freedom and spontaneity that struck white listeners as exotic and irresistible. By the end of the century, it was a craze. As minstrelsy faded, ragtime arose out of a happy convergence of circumstances: the emergence of the Negro musician, the popularity minstrelsy had established for music affected by the Negro folk tradition, the remarkable prevalence of pianos in American parlors, and the growth of an aggressive popular-music publishing industry.

The many strands of the story of ragtime are intertwined in the life of the man who deservedly came to be called "King of Ragtime," Scott Joplin (1869–1917). As a boy in Texarkana, Texas, Joplin heard the homemade music of Negro country folk, but he also learned to play the piano in a neighbor's parlor, first by ear, then from a German musician who undertook to teach him the classics of European music. At seventeen Joplin went to St. Louis to make his way as a pianist in the night club strip. There, and later in Chicago, which he visited during the

Columbian Exposition, he heard others who were beginning to shape a new style of piano-playing. In 1897, Ben Harney, a white musician famous for "clever plantation Negro imitations and excellent piano playing," brought out a book called *The Rag Time Instructor*, in which he set himself up as the "original instructor to the stage of the now popular rag time in Ethiopian song." In the same year, the first published rag by a Negro composer appeared, Tom Turpin's "Harlem Rag." Joplin himself entered the field of published ragtime early in 1899, with "Original Rags." But the flood did not really begin until September of that year, when the publisher John Stark issued the "Maple Leaf Rag." The composition took its name from the club in which Joplin was playing, in Sedalia, Missouri, when Stark heard him and offered him a contract. The piece was an immediate success, which Joplin (and Stark) followed with some three dozen other rags and an instruction book, *School of Ragtime*, published in 1908.

Joplin considered ragtime not merely an ephemeral popular music style but a new idiom for serious musical expression. He composed two operas making use of the ragtime idiom. The score of the first (*A Guest in the House*, 1903) disappeared after a concert performance in St. Louis. The failure of the second (*Treemonisha*, published by Joplin himself in 1911) in a trial performance in New York was a mortal blow for the composer. Not opera, but the "Maple Leaf Rag" assures Scott Joplin a place in American musical history.

The ragtime craze held on past the first decade of the new century. It revolutionized social dancing in the United States, and it quickly caught on in Europe when John Philip Sousa included Kerry Mills's "Georgia Camp Meeting" in the band's programs on tour there after 1900. Ironically, the most famous "ragtime" song was not a rag at all, and came not from a trained Negro composer but from a budding white songwriter who happened to be musically illiterate: "Alexander's Ragtime Band," composed in 1910 by Irving Berlin (1888——).

By that time, ragtime was good business, but the creative force that lay behind it was emerging in a new place—New Orleans. There it became a crucial strand in a web of circumstances as complicated and coincidental as that out of which ragtime itself had come. In New Orleans the music Negro musicians were inventing moved another step beyond not only minstrelsy, but also the parlor piano that was part of ragtime. And it did so by moving closer to its old southern Negro roots, though in a changed and changing South.

CONCURRENCE IN NEW ORLEANS

New Orleans at the end of the nineteenth century was the unique meeting point of an amazing assortment of historical, racial, social, religious, and musical strands. The Gordian knot of this concurrence has tantalized historians of jazz and probably will never be satisfactorily untangled.

One strand was New Orleans's background as a Spanish and French city before it was American. Its Latin-Catholic orientation set it apart from the Protestant South and created an atmosphere in which elements of the Negro's African heritage could be kept openly alive exactly at the time when they were being forced underground elsewhere. From the time of the Louisiana Purchase to the mid-1880's, a place called Congo Square (now Beauregard Square) was set aside on Sundays for New Orleans Negroes' voodoo ritual celebrations. The practices of the cult, observed in innumerable secret societies, were fed and sustained by continuing contact, through the port, with the sources of the religion in the Caribbean islands and West Africa itself. The rites in Congo Square were a tourist attraction, and accounts of witnesses, ranging from the architect Benjamin Latrobe in the early part of the century to George Washington Cable after the Civil War, testify vividly to the vigorous survival of the ecstatic drumming and incantation of West African voodoo in the midst of one of America's most cosmopolitan cities.

A second side to New Orleans's French-Spanish character was the prerogative of the men of sophisticated Creole society to take quadroon mistresses. Out of these relationships grew a caste of "gens de couleur"—Creoles of color, as they were called—who lived in the downtown quarter of the city, separate from the uptown Negroes. They were given educational opportunities usually denied Negroes; in addition to skills and trades, they often studied music, learned to play orchestral instruments, and visited the opera. Thus, at a time when it continued to offer Americans of Negro background close contact with West African musical practice, New Orleans also afforded immediate contact with European music. The barrier between the castes fell with the end of the Civil War. Increasingly from that time, in New Orleans, white was white and colored colored.

The end of the war brought another kind of American Negro into New Orleans. Emancipated slaves from ruined plantations streamed into the city to find work. They brought with them the music Negroes had fashioned on plantation and levee: the spirituals, gospel songs, and "shouts" of their religious meetings; the "hollers" and worksongs of the fields, railroads, wharves, and prisons; the singing games and dances that had been part of plantation life. All this was influenced by the musical ways of the white southerner. But slaves and former slaves had musical ways of their own, and these invested whatever they sang or played with a distinctive character and vitality.

Although Negro music first crystalized in religious songs, it found nonreligious expression as well, and in the last decades of the century it took on a musical and poetic form known as "blues." Before the war, either by choice or necessity, the Negro had kept his secular music-making within the closed circle of his own community. With slavery past, itinerant Negro musicians sang for money, strumming accompaniments on a guitar or banjo. The music was close kin to that of the spirituals. The melodies departed further from hymn patterns; perhaps they were more freely inflected with the plaintive "half cry, half yodel" of the field holler. But the phrases still fell into the four-bar regularity learned from hymns; and the guitar chords were still the faithful organ chords learned at prayer meeting, except that the musician's ear led him to echo on the stringed instrument those queer "blue" notes that he could sing but that no organ could ever play. The music was "blue," and it was also "hot" with the spiritual fervor that made the slaves' religious songs unforgettable.

The blues were a great deal closer to the roots of Negro music than ragtime was, and therefore harder for white listeners to accept. They may have been sung for decades before 1902, when "Ma" Rainey started singing them from the cabaret and then from the minstrel stage; yet she believed herself the first to sing the blues before an audience. When W. C. Handy (1873–1958) wrote his "Memphis Blues" for publication in 1910, he was conscious that he was setting down, evidently for the first time, a musical form already traditional among American Negro musicians. The "Memphis Blues" and the "St. Louis Blues," which

Shaping New Forms

followed two years later, earned Handy the title "Father of the Blues"— not of the blues as a form of folk music, but as a form of popular song.

Handy did not sing the blues, he played them on the cornet with his own band. He had graduated from playing in minstrel shows to leading a band that played for celebrations, rallies, and parades all around the southern Midwest. A good part of the music played was ragtime. Handy's was one of the countless Negro bands that sprang up in the South after the war, as bands sprouted in every part of the United States. When the Confederate armies disbanded, the instruments of their regimental bands were available free or cheap to Negroes who did not mind having a try at playing the white man's instruments.

As bands became the fashion for white communities, clubs, and organizations, they became the fashion for Negro groups too. Nowhere did the Negro bands flourish as in New Orleans. There everything was an occasion for band music—Mardi Gras festivities, political campaigns, picnics, dances, riverboat excursions, lawn parties, and especially funerals. The Negro clubs, lodges, and fraternal societies all had their brass bands. Burial societies guaranteed members a funeral procession with fitting musical accompaniment, and those who could manage membership in more than one could look forward to having a number of bands playing for their funeral.

In the last decades of the nineteenth century, some of the Creoles of color, whose work as artisans was preempted by whites, began to supplement their diminishing income by hiring out as musicians and playing in brass bands. They could play "by music," and were able to perform concert numbers and marches as well as dances popular among the Creoles—quadrilles, schottisches, mazurkas, galops, waltzes. The uptown bands played a cruder music. The musicians were untrained and could only play by ear, finding their way intuitively through familiar hymns, march tunes and popular songs. Gradually, economic necessity forced downtown Creole musicians into uptown Negro bands, and the mixing affected the playing of both. The Negro musicians who continued to play by ear learned more about their instruments and how to handle them. And the Creole musicians who wanted to fit in with the uptown bands and to please their Negro audience, including the newcomers from the countryside, had to learn to play "hot" and "blue."

There is no way of knowing what the early New Orleans brass bands sounded like, but a rich folklore has preserved some of the atmosphere of the time and place, some of the names and stories of the musicians. The Negro quarter of the city must have been pulsing with music as the bands vied with each other in "cutting" or "carving" contests—competitions to see which could draw more people to the dance or carnival it was promoting. Even the picture of the funeral procession—marching toward the cemetery to the strains of the bands' "Nearer My God to Thee," and then swinging homeward to "High Society" or "Oh, Didn't He Ramble," with the "second line" of youngsters bringing up the rear, shouting appreciation of their musical idols' newest feats or trying to imitate them on homemade instruments—has survived. Charles Bolden (*ca.* 1868–1931), who was said to have led the best of all the bands, became a legendary figure comparable to John Henry, if not Paul Bunyan. Although he could not read music, he never lost a "cutting" contest; and when he blew his horn, he could be heard for twelve miles, "calling his children home." According to "Bunk" Johnson, who played second cornet for him, "King" Bolden was "the greatest ragtime cornet player." There is no question that what-

Shaping New Forms

ever the bands played, marches, dances, hymns, popular songs, by the end of the century they all played ragtime.

The brass bands' music was street music to begin with, and it continued to be heard outdoors after the turn of the century. About that time, however, the music entered an indoor phase that brought together once and for all, in a definite configuration, all the cultural and musical threads that were parts of it. In 1897, a law was passed restricting New Orleans's many thriving vice enterprises to an area next to the old French Quarter, where entertainment parlors had years before supplanted elegant residences. Insiders called it simply "the District"; outsiders gave it the name "Storyville," after the alderman who wrote the law. By any name, the establishment meant regular work for Creole and Negro musicians who preferred to play nightly in a single spot rather than rely for their income on scattered street band jobs. There in the saloons, dance halls, brothels, and sporting houses, the new New Orleans music was heard by visitors drawn by the city's commerce and by its notoriety. They heard the ragtime bands, cornet, clarinet, and trombone freely spinning out their tunes over the sturdy pulse of banjo and drums. And they heard pianists—who, strangers to the brass bands, took their part in the music once it was indoors—demonstrate that the piano could encompass blues as well as rags. Ferdinand "Jelly Roll" Morton (1885–1941), who came from Gulfport, Louisiana, to New Orleans to earn Storyville money as a "professor" in a club run by the boss of the district, said he first used the word "jazz" in 1902. Fifteen years later when Storyville was closed down, jazz was the word that caught on to describe the music New Orleans's musicians took with them as they headed for Chicago.

By that time the mixture was complete. Spirituals, blues, and vestiges of voodoo had come together with rags, street band music, and the musical experience of Creole Negroes (an experience encompassing Spanish, Caribbean, and French folksongs and dances as well as opera and concert music). Furthermore, the new music was being taken up by white bands, like those of "Papa" Jack Laine, and was being heard beyond the confines of New Orleans, on river boats and on the vaudeville circuits. Freddie Keppard and his original Creole Band began touring in vaudeville as early as 1911, and by 1917 they had taken the new music north to the Great Lakes and from one coast to the other. It was a white band, however, led by a former Laine trombonist, that Chicagoans began talking about in 1915 when they whispered that "Tom Brown's Band from Dixieland" was playing "jazz." Given an idea that seemed to titillate the public, the manager put up a sign advertising "Brown's Dixieland Jass Band, Direct from New Orleans." The word was out in the open, and so was the music.

EXIT MINSTRELSY, ENTER MUSICAL COMEDY

Constance Rourke, writing about the decline of minstrelsy, observed that Emancipation not only freed the Negro, it freed the white from the stereotyped entertainment he had built around Jim Crow, Zip Coon, Tambo, and Bones. Both participants in minstrelsy, the Negro and the white, began to look back to their origins. As the Negro took his musical share in the entertainment back toward the South and West of its beginnings, the part of minstrelsy that stemmed from the English theater turned back toward "variety" and toward Britain and Europe. The minstrel show had, after all, started from the circus and variety acts of traveling players, a good many of them British players. As the Civil War ended, there was a resurgence of variety entertainment which, taking a fresh form, gradually took over the minstrel show's place in the New York theaters that set the direction for the American musical stage. At the same time, productions of the musical stage of England and the Continent were received with heightened enthusiasm.

As minstrelsy weakened and declined, one new form after another was tried on the American musical stage, as if producers were seeking something that would capture the public's fancy as minstrelsy had done. The search brought forth a number of remarkably successful productions and in the process gradually shaped new forms for American musical theater in general. Musically, however, there appeared no fresh American idiom to succeed that of fading minstrelsy.

New theatrical efforts followed lines stemming from minstrelsy's two Anglo-European sources: the variety show and the European musical stage. It had clear new beginnings, with Tony Pastor (1837–1908) in the one case, and with *The Black Crook* in the other.

Tony Pastor, born in New York City, began as a professional entertainer in his childhood and became acquainted with every aspect of mid-century American entertainment. He played tambourine in a minstrel show; he traveled with eight different circus troupes in roles ranging from comic singer to bareback rider; and he performed in the kind of variety show that was gaining popularity in the saloons of the Bowery. Pastor took the measure of the theater-going public and decided that if minstrelsy could be made acceptable as family entertainment, so could the topical song-dance-comedy of variety. In 1866, after trying out the idea in Paterson, New Jersey, he opened a new showplace in the Bowery, to be not a saloon, but an "Opera House." The nickname offered assurance that here would be found entertainment wives could enjoy, unblushing, with their husbands. Pastor further lured the ladies with such innocent door prizes as dress patterns, kitchen goods, and coal. The family trade came. In the next decade and a half Pastor moved twice to larger theaters. By the time he built his Music Hall on Union Square in 1891, vaudeville was established as a form of American theater.

Though the relationship was strong and clear between the "olio" of the minstrel show (the medley of monologues, songs, skits, and dances that made up the second of the traditional minstrel presentation's three parts) and the loose succession of numbers that made up an evening at Pastor's, the new variety entertainments represented a break with minstrelsy. They opened the way for the musical stage to explore the possibilities of other American characters than the Negro. The American Irishman, German, Italian, Jew, and Chinese, as well as Negro were represented in the New York scene of the "Mulligan" shows which Edward N. Harrigan (1845–1911) and his partner Tony Hart (1857–91) presented in the 1870's and 1880's. Both Harrigan and Hart were former minstrel performers, and the farces they built around the comic antics of the members of the "Mulligan Guard" resembled the olio of a minstrel show with locale shifted from exotic plantation life to the Bowery. In changing the scene and giving the succession of song, dance, and novelty numbers a unifying theme taken from contemporary everyday life, Harrigan and Hart started the musical theater's move from minstrelsy to musical revue.

With *The Brook*, which appeared in New York in 1879 (the same year as the first full-length Mulligan show), Nate Salisbury had already taken a further step. *The Brook* dealt with homely materials and situations, as Harrigan (and, indeed, minstrelsy) did, but it hung these on the thin thread of a plot. In trying to reproduce naturally, in a musical farce, "the jollity and funny mishaps that attend in the usual pic-nic excursion," Salisbury felt *The Brook* was "different in its motive and execution from any musical production of its kind thus far presented for public consideration."

While *The Brook* in some ways hit upon the direction in which musical comedy would develop, it did not have an original score. In fact, none of these new ventures could claim any musical distinction. The shows in Pastor's Music Hall and their off-shoots in vaudeville and burlesque-extravaganza were simply showcases for the stars of the day singing topical songs or current popular ballads. That these included the type then widely (if crudely) known as "coon songs" was a tribute to the continuing hold of the old minstrel idiom on public favor, not to any fresh creative impulse. In pre-Mulligan days, Harrigan and Hart sang "Walkin' for Dat Cake" by David Braham (1838–1905); and in the Mulligan shows, they continued to present songs written by the London-born Braham in good British music-hall style.

The form of musical farce comedy popularized by Harrigan and Hart reached its peak of popularity in the 1890's with Charles Hoyt's *A Trip to Chinatown*. The play's thread of a plot was homely enough—adventures of two couples slumming in San Francisco; and its topical comedy touched on such things as the temperance crusade and woman suffrage. The music, however, was written by British-born Percy Gaunt (d. 1896), who for a time had been musical director for Harrigan and Hart. If the hit of the show, "The Bowery," is a genuine piece of Americana, only the words have made it so; Sigmund Spaeth has traced its waltzing tune to an English, even a Neapolitan, source.

American Music

Lacking native musical flavor, shows often sought to win an audience by approaching the audience's everyday life. The opposite appeal defined *The Black Crook*, which opened with spectacular success in New York City in 1866. A melange of Romantic ballet, melodrama, and sheer stage spectacle, *The Black Crook* evoked gasps of wonder for its final "transformation scene" and drew mixed delight and outrage for its lavish display of tights-clad female legs.

It was the product of a curious chain of circumstances. Two young impresarios had undertaken to bring a French ballet company to perform at the Academy of Music. Before the troupe could perform, but after it had arrived in New York with a full array of fancy scenery and costumes, the Academy burned down. The managers, in search of a stage, turned to Niblo's Garden, where the manager was preparing a none too promising melodrama, *The Black Crook* by Charles Barras. Someone determined to combine the ballet and the melodrama in one great extravaganza. And so, with the most elaborate production machinery that could be devised, they did. F. L. Ritter attributed the success of *The Black Crook* to the fact that "a certain class of men, suddenly enriched by speculation," had begun to influence the character of public entertainment as "on the strength of their suddenly acquired riches, the sensuous side of the nature of these people began to clamor for adequate food."

In any case, its appeal was sophisticated enough to reach the fashionable audience of the opera, popular enough to lure the friends of minstrelsy and the Bowery. Ministers and a newspaper or two branded it "indecent." But the ballet and the sheer elaborateness of the production seemed to justify attending in the name of Art, and the extravaganza's popularity left no doubt that one had to attend in the name of Fashion. In its first production, *The Black Crook* ran for sixteen months in 474 performances, and it was far from finished then. It cropped up during the next twenty-five years in a variety of revivals in and outside New York and received the tribute of numerous imitations.

The contribution of *The Black Crook* to American music was nil; its score was simply strung together from a number of sources by Niblo's musical director, Giuseppe Operti. But it was Broadway's first long-run musical show, and it suggested the production pattern later American theater pieces would follow. Instead of introducing new works into the repertoire of a permanent company, a new company would be assembled for each new show, with the aim of playing it as long as possible on Broadway and then taking it "on the road." In the range of the public it attracted and in the mixture of theatrical elements it brought together, *The Black Crook* was also anticipatory. It was followed by a whole series of musical spectacles which contributed to the development of American stagecraft, if not to the development of American music.

Between the Civil War and the turn of the century, the vein of variety and farce-comedy brought the American musical stage closer to realism and the vernacular, and the vein of extravaganza succeeded in broadening the range of both its technical resources and its audience. To bring the two together and integrate them with equally adept and lively music appeared beyond the capacities of the place and time. The audience, or that part of it inclined toward such things, could only view with covetous admiration the examples of *opéra bouffe* (Offenbach, Lecocq) or of blossoming Viennese operetta (Suppe, Johann Strauss, Jr.) offered by visiting French companies or in German language theaters in the 1870's and 1880's.

American Music

A Boston shipping clerk named Edward E. Rice decided to produce an "American opera bouffe" that would be in English and more wholesome than some of the racy French comedies. The result was *Evangeline*, a homespun burlesque of Longfellow which opened at Niblo's Garden in 1874 and became a perennial favorite throughout the country during the next thirty years. A contemporary reviewer described its music as "light, ballad-like, a trifle lively," but said it "cannot compare in sprightliness to the dullest opera bouffe." Indeed, Rice was no composer; he played the piano by ear and set his tunes down in a private musical shorthand for transcription by a professional musician. Nevertheless, he produced in *Evangeline* the first full-length piece of American popular musical theater with a completely original score.

Rice himself developed doubts about calling *Evangeline* an opéra bouffe, and later decided "American extravaganza" described it better. He aimed, he said, "to foster a taste for musical comedy relieved of the characteristic and objectionable features of opera bouffe." Besides telling us something about *Evangeline*, Rice's statement is notable for its early use of the term "musical comedy" in the modern sense.

With the arrival of *H. M. S. Pinafore* in 1878, Americans for the first time sensed the possibilities of light opera in English. There was then no copyright agreement to protect the work of Gilbert and Sullivan in the United States, so *Pinafore* was pirated in a Boston performance six months after its premier in London. *Pinafore* troupes sprang up quickly all over the country and the piece had been performed hundreds of times before Richard d'Oyly Carte brought the authentic article to New York in 1879. Arthur Sullivan himself conducted the opening performance, with W. S. Gilbert in the ship's crew. American producers had no chance to beat d'Oyly Carte to the draw with the next

Shaping New Forms

Gilbert and Sullivan success. *Pirates of Penzance* was given its premiere by the British company in New York on New Year's Eve 1879.

The whole succession of Savoy operas found a ready audience in the United States, and an increasing number of French and Viennese operettas were given fancy productions in English translation. Americans were bound to try their hand at it, and soon did. John Philip Sousa (1854–1932), perhaps spurred by his experience as violinist in Offenbach's orchestra at Philadelphia in 1876, made his first (unsuccessful) attempt as early as 1879. He went on to write at least ten more light operas, some of which were moderately successful in the 1890's. *El Capitan* (1896), generally considered his best, is still remembered, but only because of the march that bears its title. Sousa's masterpiece was "The Stars and Stripes Forever," not an operetta. Reginald de Koven (1859–1920) wrote some twenty operettas between 1887 and 1913, but only *Robin Hood* (1890) is faintly remembered for the song "O Promise Me."

Several American composers of concert music ventured out of their element to try emulating Sullivan or Strauss, but the idiom did not come easily to Dudley Buck, Edgar Stillman Kelley (1857–1944) or George Whitefield Chadwick, as their unsuccessful *Deseret* (1880), *Puritania* (1892), and *Tabasco* (1894) respectively proved. Operetta required a particular knack, and the first American enduringly distinguished by it was Victor Herbert (1859–1924). Born in Ireland and trained in Germany, Herbert was brought to New York from Stuttgart in 1886 as part of a package Frank Damrosch (Walter's older brother) contracted for when he engaged the soprano Therese Foerster for the new German opera at the Metropolitan. Miss Foerster, soon Mrs. Herbert, was a star; Herbert was cellist in the orchestra. Herbert went on to conduct Gilmore's Band after the founder's death and then to conduct the Pittsburgh Symphony, at the same time making a name for himself as composer of light but well-made concert music.

Herbert's first operetta, *Prince Ananias*, came out in 1894, and he began to achieve some success with *The Serenade* (1897) and *The Fortune Teller* (1898). But his best-remembered works came after the turn of the century. In the 1890's, the light opera laurels in America went to imported works. Most popular of all was the now-forgotten *Erminie*, brought from London in 1886. Edward Jacobowski wrote the score for the piece, which took its plot from an old French farce. With a fancy pink ballroom scene as one of its chief attractions, *Erminie* was performed more than a thousand times in New York before the end of the century.

The reigning star of the American comic opera stage during those years, Miss Lillian Russell, was heard mainly in British operettas, occasionally in one from Paris or Vienna. And the first operetta to have New York as its setting, *The Belle of New York* by German-born, Louisville-reared Gustave Kerker (1857–1923), found more favor in London than in New York, where it was introduced in 1897. Even in the realm of the leg-show extravaganza and farce comedy, visiting British troupes repeatedly outshone American productions, from the high-kicking blonds of Lydia Thompson's *Ixion* in 1868 through *The Gaiety Girl* of 1894 to *Florodora* in 1900.

As the new century opened, the beginnings of an American synthesis appeared. The shows produced by George M. Cohan (1878–1942) brought together elements of the different kinds of entertainment the musical stage had been trying out, combining them in a racy new kind of show for which only the term "musical comedy" seemed apt.

Like Tony Pastor, Cohan grew up in the American entertainment world. As one of the Four Cohans, he was playing the variety circuit with his parents and sister from one side of the country to the other before he was thirteen. By the time he was sixteen, he had published his first song and was writing a good part of the material for the Cohans' skits. Dissatisfied with the loose variety format, he began, at the turn of the century, to experiment with the idea of expanding the usual brief skeches into full-length musical comedies. After two unsuccessful attempts, he found the combination he sought in *Little Johnny Jones*, in 1904. Cohan wrote the book and the music for this play, which took an American jockey to England to ride for the King (as the real-life jockey, Tod Sloane, had done the year before). Two songs in the show have become part of American folklore: "Give My Regards to Broadway" and "The Yankee Doodle Boy." Within two years, Cohan had two new shows running simultaneously on Broadway. While *Forty-five Minutes from Broadway* was introducing the sleepy village of New Rochelle and "Mary's a Grand Old Name" in one theater, Cohan himself was wrapping himself in the Stars and Stripes and singing "You're a Grand Old Flag" as the star of *George Washington Jr.* in another.

There was more in these musical plays than flag-waving and sentimentalism about Broadway. With them, Cohan coined a kind of hard-boiled, fast-moving, brash, cocky, vernacular entertainment that American audiences recognized as their own. In a long and colorful career, Cohan wrote dozens of shows, in which he combined stagecraft learned from extravaganza and operetta with the topical, down-to-earth subject matter and humor of variety and farce-comedy. A reviewer wrote of one Cohan show that it went so fast it gave "the impression of a great machine shooting out characters, choruses, songs, dances, with rapidfire quickness and precision." It was such a machine that Finley Peter Dunne had in mind when he had Mr. Dooley say, "When we Americans get through with the English language, it will look as if it had been run over by a musical comedy."

Minstrelsy, along with the frontier and plantation life, was past. With Cohan, a new native form and style had arrived. Yet while Cohan's stagecraft was unchallenged, his music consisted of songs written more to attain Tin-Pan Alley popularity than to develop plot or character. To the elements he had combined, only time and greater talents would bring maturity.

Part Three

EMERGENCE

VII

Bridge to the Present

A period beginning just before World War I and extending into the 1920's seems to mark the transition between past and present in American musical life. During that period, lines of development from the previous half-century were affected by new factors of such significance that what resulted seemed almost a new order of things. Before, the country's musical practice was based on a complex of borrowed, adapted, improvised, invented musical institutions that still largely reflected (with distortions) the musical culture of Germany and England. After, an American musical culture clearly had emerged.

The direction of change had already been set. Almost from the start, America's musical development had been affected by two distinctive crosscurrents. On the one hand, Anglo-European and Afro-American musical practices interacted with each other; on the other, the interplay of those two great tendencies, the one elevating, the other broadening, that stemmed from the democratic cast of the country had its impact. The musical product of these and the social forces at work in America emerged distinctly now, in the span of a few transforming years. The growing importance of urban as against rural living, the intensified sense of national identity, the spirit of democratic reform abroad in the land were bound to show in its evolving musical institutions and practices—had, in fact, already affected them. But the process of change, suddenly compressed, was no longer gradual but acute. In the second and third decades of the new century, the two distinctive crosscurrents of the country's musical development, hitherto submerged, broke through to the surface as the characteristic features of American musical life. And the precipitating factors were the phonograph, the radio, and the Great War. The two new media perfectly suited the farflung American musical audience that had taken shape in the nineteenth century. They affected every phase of the country's musical life, but none more than jazz, which largely through them almost immediately transcended its local origins and became a national idiom. The war broke finally the hold of the German classical tradition on American musical standards. It spurred both musicians and audiences to open themselves to fresh influences and at the same time it prompted a new awareness and acceptance of America's own musical resources.

That broadening-elevating tendency in American musical life, identified at the start with the colonial singing schools, persisted in the twentieth century, a dauntless combination of musical (and business) enterprise and missionary spirit. In the growing cities, music was seen as a means of social advancement among the immigrants and poor, and neighborhood music classes were carried on by the latest generation of spiritual descendants of the

Bridge to the Present

old singing masters. Frank Damrosch (1859–1937), Walter's brother, gave up supervising public school music in Denver to establish People's Singing Classes in New York in the 1890's. There the "working-man" was taught to read notes, to sing his part in a chorus, and ultimately to participate in performances of "the greatest works of the greatest masters." The classes soon found an echo in other communities, and similar groups met in settlement houses or in school buildings, which everywhere were beginning to take on the nature of community centers.

In the schools themselves, music instruction now commonly ventured beyond singing from the songbooks of Lowell Mason and his disciples to include band and orchestra classes. And when Frank Damrosch began conducting the New York Symphony Society in a regular series of Concerts for Young People in 1898, the children who came had been prepared by their classroom teachers to hear the music explained and performed.

By the time war broke out in Europe, the musical movement centering in the school and neighborhood center had reached national proportions and embraced outdoor festivals, municipal concerts and community choruses singing in school auditoriums and parks. During the war years these activities furnished a basis for programs more concerned with morale than with music. Community singing took over and "the world's great music" found itself drowned out by George M. Cohan's "Over There" and a parcel of war songs from England that included "Pack Up Your Troubles," "It's a Long Way to Tipperary," and "Keep the Home Fires Burning." It was a happy day for the community singers when someone discovered that the last song could be sung together—in counterpoint!—with "There's a Long, Long Trail A-Winding," written a few years earlier by a Yale student, Alonzo Elliott.

American Music

After the war, community music efforts redoubled. Music had proved its worth "as a force in citizenship building and community morale" (echoes of Lowell Mason), and so new support was forthcoming from civic groups and even from municipal governments. Ukulele clubs played on corner playgrounds, employees' bands rehearsed in factories, and community sings were held in city parks across the country. Outgrowths of the movement were new outdoor music programs at Lewisohn Stadium in New York (1918), at the Hollywood Bowl (1922), and at the Cincinnati Zoo, where in 1921 an open air opera stage took the place of the old bandstand. The number of permanent symphony orchestras continued to grow throughout the war. Of the two dozen major American orchestras playing in 1960, six had been founded before the turn of the century; half the remainder were established between 1900 and 1920, in cities as widespread as Philadelphia and Los Angeles, Minneapolis and Houston. Unlike the opera, which tended to cling to its plutocratic tradition, the orchestras sought and found a place for themselves in community life. They gave concerts for children and concerts for workers. And gradually the basis of their financial support broadened. Though many orchestras owed their existence to an endowment established by a single benefactor, paternalistic sponsorship patterned on Boston's Higginson model gradually gave way to voluntary financial support from an increasingly wide musical public.

The pioneering of the nineteenth century's musical missionaries had created that public; it existed everywhere, without geographic or social distinction, well before radio appeared on the scene to respond to its appetite. Even before the turn of the century, members of a chamber music group traveling across the country found audiences so much alike, "We cannot tell whether

Bridge to the Present

we are playing in Bangor or Omaha or on the Pacific coast." In music, as otherwise, frontier days were past. In mid-nineteenth century, Theodore Thomas and William Mason had stood out on the street passing out leaflets to lure New Yorkers into a chamber music concert. Between 1905 and 1930, the Flonzaley String Quartette found audiences for a hundred concerts a year in four hundred cities.

A new generation of traveling virtuosi toured the country with comfort and acclaim—Paderewski, Rachmaninoff, Kubelik, Casals, Rosenthal, Lhevinne, de Pachmann, Ysaye, the boy Mischa Elman, and the Americans Albert Spaulding, Maud Powell, Olga Samaroff (née Hickenlooper). Singers such as Enrico Caruso, John McCormack, Louise Homer, and Geraldine Farrar were heard in every part of the country, if not with the Metropolitan Opera during its weeks on tour, then in concert. The Metropolitan's complacently conventional repertoire and staging ironically served to broaden available musical resources. Oscar Hammerstein built the Manhattan Opera House in 1906, and with a brilliant company of singers gave the old-line Met serious competition for four venturesome years. When Hammerstein was bought off by the Metropolitan's management in 1910, the company moved to Chicago as the Philadelphia-Chicago Opera. In its succeeding forms, as Chicago Opera or Chicago Civic Opera, the company (artistically dominated by the soprano Mary Garden and the conductor Cleofonte Campanini) not only established first-rate opera in the Midwest, but through touring, and through the concert appearances of its singers, brought opera and its performers before a growing audience.

It was inevitable that someone should organize that audience, and the initiative came in 1920 from the manager of Redpath's Chautauqua and Lyceum Bureau in Chicago, Harry P. Harrison.

American Music

He had been organizing lecture courses for community groups and clubs in towns throughout the Midwest. Now he applied his experience to concert courses. In numbers of small towns around Chicago, he found or formed groups interested in hearing leading musical artists; then he arranged for the artists to make the circuit of his ready-made audiences. No financial risk was involved; each course was fully subscribed in advance, on a nonprofit basis, by the community group that would attend the concerts. The first season's experimental "All-Star Series" worked. When in 1921 Harrison formed a partnership with Dema Harshbarger to promote the formation of what now were to be called "Civic Music Associations," the organized audience plan became part of the American music business. Grasping the size of the potential public for concerts in outlying communities as well as in the larger cities, a group of New York managers, led by Arthur Judson, decided to secure that audience for their artist-clients through the organized audience plan. In 1928 they formed the Community Concerts Corporation. In the ensuing decades, the organized audience movement expanded, suffered Depression setbacks, and expanded again until, in the 1950's, two major "concert services" were providing yearly musical programs to organized audience groups in 1,900 communities in every part of the country.

PHONOGRAPH AND RADIO

The phonograph had begun to whet and satisfy the musical appetites of America's farflung audiences years before anyone thought of organizing them. From the early years of the century, owners of Thomas Edison's phonographs (which played cylinders) or of Emil Berliner's gramophones or Eldridge Johnson's Victrolas (both of which played discs), or indeed any of the

Bridge to the Present

competing "graphophones" or "talking machines," could hear in their homes the voices of leading opera singers and music hall entertainers of the day. By 1920 the recording companies offered extracts from larger instrumental works, band music, even parts of symphonies.

In the schools, records had already begun to take their place alongside songbooks as a music teacher's tool. The Victor Talking Machine Company saw the possibilities early, and in 1911 established a special department to make the electrical instrument "a means of real education." Under Francis E. Clark's direction, recordings were prepared to help the teacher impart the fundamentals of music through excerpts from classics as well as school songs, folksongs, and folkdances. Mrs. Clark's book, *Music Appreciation for Children*, published by Victor, was a pioneer effort in its field. In the next decade, several books were published to "explain" the recorded music to adults as well. *The Victor Book of the Opera* and *What We Hear in Music* discussed the workings of symphonies, operas, and concert pieces, not in the abstract, nor with reference to scores, but in terms of specific recorded performances.

In 1919, the record industry was booming. More than two million phonographs were produced, and sales of records were approaching a hundred million a year. The next year, radio broadcasting began.

If ever an audience and a medium were made for each other, it was the American musical audience and radio. This audience had learned hymn tunes, Handel melodies, and folksongs out of the same books; it had seen a minstrel show one night and an opera the next in the same theater; it had heard Caruso and Sousa on the phonograph, ragtime and Chopin on the player piano, Wagner and polkas, Verdi and quadrilles from the town band.

American Music

It was an audience without musical prejudices and with a taste for many different things, including the best music. It was, in short, the first mass audience that had existed for professional musical performance. In radio, it found a mass medium to serve it.

By 1914 Arthur Farwell sensed not the outcome, but the character of the new situation created by the interaction of "musical art and democracy"—the emergence of "a wholly new and multifold phase of musical life." But in Farwell's thinking, it was the community and neighborhood musical activity then gaining momentum throughout the country that was most important. The role to be filled by that obscure, experimental device called "radio" did not enter his mind. Two years later, however, David Sarnoff, who was working with radio, had a glimmer of what was to come. In a letter to his superiors at the Marconi Wireless Telegraph Company, he proposed manufacturing "radio music boxes" which would bring centrally broadcast musical programs into their owners' homes. Sarnoff estimated that within three years sales of such sets could amount to $75,000,000—an estimate proved almost exactly correct some years later. But preoccupied with problems of developing radio for commercial communications, the radio companies were not ready in 1916 to think of it as entertainment.

When in 1920 radio broadcasting finally began, music immediately became a mainstay. Dr. Frank Conrad of the Westinghouse Company, experimenting with transmission equipment in a room above his garage in Pittsburgh, tired of talking into his microphone and began sending out recorded music instead. To his surprise, he began receiving letters and telephone calls from amateurs who were receiving his broadcasts, asking him to play some particular record or to broadcast at a particular time of day. There were other unexpected results. The dealer from

Bridge to the Present

whom Conrad borrowed records for his programs reported that a growing number of customers were coming in to buy records that had been broadcast. The Westinghouse company had already begun to note a rise in sales of parts used in making home receivers when in September 1920 a Pittsburgh department store began advertising ready-made sets to bring "Dr. Conrad's popular broadcasts" into any home. Westinghouse's vice-president, H. P. Davis, saw what David Sarnoff had seen four years earlier, and took action. Radio station KDKA was built to send out regular radio programs to receivers in people's homes. Conceived as both a service to the public and a stimulus to the sale of radio equipment, the station made its debut broadcasting the results of the presidential election November 2, 1920.

The statistics are familiar. In 1922 there were radio sets in sixty thousand American homes and thirty stations broadcasting. Five years later nearly seven million homes were receiving broadcasts from nearly seven hundred stations. Radio simply swept the country, with the irresistible appeal of a magical new medium and free entertainment right in the parlor. Part of the fun of it was to see how many stations the family receiver could pull in, and from how far away.

A good part of it was music. When the National Broadcasting Company introduced network radio in 1926, ten million tuned in to hear a musical program that ranged from the New York Symphony and Oratorio Society to the Goldman Band and an array of dance orchestras.

Indeed the dance orchestra virtually took over the airwaves. Detroit's WWJ had broadcast Paul Specht's band "live" from its studio in September, 1920. Within a few years, Vincent Lopez and Paul Whiteman were broadcasting, along with Ted Lewis, Isham Jones, Abe Lyman, Ben Bernie, Ted Weems, Rudy Vallee, and others, as radio tried to satisfy the "roaring '20's" passion for dance music. By 1928, America's radio audience had passed twenty million. Though the practice of selling radio time for advertising was barely under way, radio programmers viewed broadcasting largely as a means of promoting the sale of their equipment, and they were careful to broadcast what the public wanted to have. In seeking to widen their audience, they were led more and more to dance music. A survey of ten large radio stations in these early years showed that 85 per cent of their broadcast time was given over to music, and that for every hour of concert or operatic music, there were six hours of "harmony and rhythm" or "syncopation."

Though concert music's role in radio turned out to be smaller than some hoped, radio's role in concert music was not negligible. Walter Damrosch began broadcasting a weekly "Music Appreciation Hour" in 1928, and in the next decade the NBC network was reaching an audience of some seven million school children through a program that was part of the regular curriculum in seventy thousand schools. In 1930, the CBS network offered Sunday afternoon concerts of the Philharmonic-Symphony Society of New York, turning a local institution into a national one. For a time the Metropolitan Opera resisted the microphone. When the Chicago Civic Opera broadcast the garden scene from *Faust* in 1928, a Metropolitan spokesman disdained to consider it an opera performance. But by 1931, the Met's management was so hard pressed financially that it allowed itself to be lured by NBC's substantial offer (perhaps as much as $100,000) into a series of broadcasts beginning with a Christmas performance of *Hansel and Gretel*. Two years later, in an apparently mortal financial pinch, the Metropolitan turned to the nationwide radio audience with its first public appeal for funds. Financial need thus

Bridge to the Present

forced the transformation of the Metropolitan from an exclusive private institution to a public one, and because of radio, a public one national in scope. When in 1940 the Metropolitan Opera Association launched a campaign to buy its opera house, a third of the one million dollars raised came from the radio audience. The advent of radio signaled hard times for the phonograph record industry. Eventually the development of the electrical recording process helped it to recover. But in the early 1920's, the zooming popularity of radio was an important factor in a decline of as much as 85 per cent in record sales. The business was saved from total bankruptcy by the popular dance music craze and by a growing demand for what the trade called "Race Recordings." These were mainly blues of an undiluted variety not to be heard on the radio.

Southern Negroes moving into large northern cities formed a ready market for recordings of the kind of music they had left behind. When a new Bessie Smith recording went on sale in Clarence Williams's record shop on Chicago's South Side in the mid-1920's, customers would line up around the block to buy it, and when the shop's stock ran out, there was a thriving trade in the back alleys at higher prices. Together Negro migration and phonograph records effected the dissemination of jazz, from the South to the rest of the country, and from Negro to white players and audiences.

Ironically, the first jazz recordings, in 1917, were made by a group of white players, the Original Dixieland Jazz Band, who had just come from New Orleans to play at Reisenweber's restaurant in New York. Their music was so novel that the management had to tell the customers it was meant for dancing. Six years later Joe Oliver and his Creole Orchestra, having moved to Chicago, recorded the sound of New Orleans music as its

145

inventors played it. Meanwhile, young white musicians were buying "ODJB" records and copying them. Leon ("Bix") Beiderbecke, in Davenport, Iowa, modeled his playing after the cornetist Nick La Rocca's. The Chicago boys who made up the Austin High School Gang painstakingly copied recorded performances of the New Orleans Rhythm Kings, another white group up from the South, just as a few years later, in Spokane, Washington, Bing Crosby haunted a record shop to hear and model his singing after the "hot" playing of the (white) Mound City Blue Blowers. To listen to Negro players, young jazz addicts visited Chicago's Negro dance halls, where they listened in awe to "King" Oliver and his second cornetist, Louis Armstrong. Too young to go in, "Muggsy" Spanier sat outside on the curb catching what he could of the music.

As northern white players took it over, the music changed. Chicago jazz differed from the original New Orleans style, and the style of Beiderbecke's Wolverines (who began playing for campus dances in 1923) differed from everything within range. But the music was also changing among Negro musicians. As jazz moved from New Orleans, it left its folk origins further and further behind. As soloists of the brilliance and personality of Louis Armstrong (1900——) emerged, the steady ensemble playing of old New Orleans style gave way to more extended solos set against a blended background. There was a tendency, too, to cater to the preference of dancers for larger bands. Jelly Roll Morton was probably the first to write out arrangements for a small jazz group's performance (though, as he noted, jazz is "playing more music than you can put on paper"). In the mid-1920's, Fletcher Henderson (1898–1952) formed a big band (ten players—twice the size of an ordinary jazz group) in New York, and with Don Redman created a new art of arranging for it, an art

Bridge to the Present

conceived to synchronize the sections while giving rein to soloists like Armstrong and Coleman Hawkins, to preserve the vigor of jazz while satisfying the dancers. A few years later, in 1927, the band of Edward Kennedy Ellington attracted attention when it moved into Harlem's Cotton Club. A trained musician who had never been to New Orleans, "Duke" Ellington (1899———) played an original brand of composed music; it was scored for dance orchestra yet was based unmistakably on jazz feeling, "hot" style, and the blues. By 1927, "New Orleans Jazz" was virtually a thing of the past. Jazz musicians were trying new techniques, sometimes for economic reasons, sometimes for musical. The music was already tending in a direction that would in the next decade give rise to "swing."

GEORGE GERSHWIN: FADING BOUNDARIES

Even in 1924, when New Orleans jazz was at its peak of vitality, inspiring new developments in New York and Kansas City, it was flourishing in a milieu that could be found in every part of the country and yet was limited. Outside of records (which were not yet plentiful), it was to be heard in Negro dance halls, a few speakeasies, and at semiprivate "rent parties," where Negro pianists in Chicago and New York were beginning to take off from ragtime into new styles of playing called "stride" and "boogie-woogie." Most Americans were scarcely aware of all this. "Jazz" was a word with forbidden overtones, to some titillating, to others repellent, and was familiar only in occasional "hot" solos that varied the blandly bouncing music of popular dance bands in hotels, theaters, and restaurants across the country.

Most popular of all were the bands of Paul Whiteman (1890–

147

American Music

1967), nineteen of them, representing a million-dollar-a-year business. In 1923, Whiteman took one of his bands to Europe and there met a response to his "symphonic syncopation" which suggested that his American music was undervalued in his own land. When he came home, he set about correcting the situation. He began planning a concert to be given in prestigious Aeolian Hall in New York before an audience including the most distinguished musical figures of the day. He would show in the concert how far America's "syncopated music" (the word jazz was to be used with caution) had been brought from its primitive origins.

The relationship between jazz and musical art was a subject that piqued imaginations almost from the time the new music began to be heard outside New Orleans. Europeans thought about it before Americans did. Taking his inspiration from some American sheet music Ernest Ansermet brought to him in Paris, Igor Stravinsky wrote *Ragtime for Eleven Instruments* in 1918, before he had even heard a jazz band. At that time, the jazz environment on its home ground was scarcely conducive to thoughts of art. Jimmy McPartland (one of the Austin High alumni) recalled trying to play on as if unconcerned in one of Chicago's Prohibition-era night clubs, as gangsters wielding smashed whiskey bottles "made mincemeat out of people" before his eyes. But in the same era, Bix Beiderbecke studied scores of Debussy, Stravinsky, Delius, Cyril Scott, and a now-forgotten American composer named Eastwood Lane (1879–1951). The clarinetist Pee Wee Russell remembered that after hearing Rudolph Ganz conduct the *Firebird Suite* in a St. Louis Symphony concert, Bix asked why a jazz band should not be able to make use of ideas like those heard there. He saw no reason why any musical effect or device should be exclusively "classical" or "popular." Music, for him, was not to be forced into narrow compartments.

Bridge to the Present

In exploring what traditional music might contribute to the vocabulary of jazz, Bix Beiderbecke anticipated by nearly a quarter of a century the "modern jazz" musicians. But the more prevalent question in earlier days was whether jazz might contribute something to the vocabulary of traditional music. There were two reasons to hope that the answer might be affirmative: first, it would be a distinctively American contribution and thus balm to America's feelings of cultural inferiority; and second, freed of the taint of brothel and speakeasy, jazz would become respectable and thus more lucrative for dance bands.

No one hoped these two hopes more fervently than the "king of jazz," Paul Whiteman. The details of Whiteman's "Experiment in Modern Music" of February 12, 1924, have often been told. A distinguished Aeolian Hall audience including Walter Damrosch, Fritz Kreisler, Sergei Rachmaninoff, and Leopold Stokowski was regaled with a long program in which the closest approach to jazz came in the first number, a version of "Livery Stable Blues" intended to show how comically primitive jazz had been ten years before. Despite the deliberate burlesque, Olin Downes, reviewing the concert for the *New York Times*, found the first piece better than the "polite" music that followed. For two reasons, however, the concert was historically important. First, it established plainly that America had developed a new kind of popular music—music that was not itself jazz (which in its most authentic forms would never be widely popular), but that was affected by the pulse and inflection of jazz. Second, it introduced (near the end of the program), a new work called *Rhapsody in Blue*, in which George Gershwin sought to express himself in an extended and serious composition using the idioms of that popular music.

Gershwin (1898–1937) and the *Rhapsody in Blue* derived from, represented, and extended a musical culture in which the line between "popular" and "classical" was becoming less and less relevant. For years, great quantities of American missionary energy had gone into making the "classics" popular. They had been explained and analyzed before audiences of children and workers. They had been excerpted, simplified, and set to words. They had been sung and played (or attempted) in neighborhood centers and by school bands. In radio broadcasts they had been preceded and followed indiscriminately by the latest in dance melodies. They were thus widely known but no longer heard exclusively amid the decorum and formality of concert hall or opera house. They were heard in the home, in the park, in the theater, just as popular music was. What underlay the symphonic ambition of *Rhapsody in Blue* was not middle-class longing for respectability but the democratic conviction that what was popular could also be fine.

The musical quality of the *Rhapsody* has long been debated by critics. Whatever the work's technical weaknesses and how-ever distant it is from jazz, it still vividly embodies those large converging currents of the country's musical development: the American encounter of European and Negro musics, and the simultaneously rising and broadening tendencies of the demo-cratic tradition.

Gershwin's earliest ambition was "to be a great popular-song composer," and even his early efforts showed so much talent that the concert singer Eva Gauthier, who liked to include the new and experimental in her programs, sang a group of Gersh-win songs in her Aeolian Hall recital several months before Whiteman's concert. The success of that venture and of the Whiteman concert prompted Walter Damrosch to ask Gershwin to compose a piano concerto.

From that time, Gershwin's success as a composer for Broadway (and later, for films) and as a composer of concert music was conspicuous. He wrote the scores of more than a dozen shows, half of them "hits." And he composed a handful of concert works that remain in the repertoire. His youthful aim to become a great songwriter he unquestionably achieved. His later ambition, to create larger musical forms in the idiom of his songs, was loftier and so more hazardous. The best pages of the *Rhapsody in Blue*, the *Concerto in F*, and *An American in Paris*, however, embody a fine impudence and a nostalgia well beyond the capacity of show tunes. They remain an expression of Gershwin and his time that may well prove timeless.

Gershwin's last work, the opera *Porgy and Bess*, was his most ambitious. It was produced in 1935, not in an opera house, but in the theater, and like the *Rhapsody* and the *Concerto*, it stirred controversy. Was it opera? Was it a musical show? Was it folk music? Was it art? The lines between categories had indeed begun to blur.

SYNTHESIS IN THE THEATER

Musical comedy had seemed, in the first decade of the century, on the verge of achieving a synthesis of its own. By the late 1920's the synthesis was achieved with the help of the dance craze and the jazz-affected popular music that engendered and accompanied it.

The American musical theater had always leaned toward realism and the vernacular, from the early days of ballad opera down through the minstrel shows, Harrigan and Hart, and George M. Cohan. Action and speech from everyday life were already the stuff of musical comedy; only a true musical vernacular was wanting. In the idiom of popular dance music, musicians found musical speech as pertinent to the life and talk of urban America as that of the minstrels had been to the life of frontier America.

The huge success of Franz Lehar's operetta *The Merry Widow* in New York in 1907 seemed to banish forever the stereotyped drills and acrobatics that had been serving as dance numbers in American musical productions. The answer to Lehar's Viennese waltzes was not, however, American waltzes, but the fox-trot, the ragtime one-step, and the tango as Vernon and Irene Castle danced them to Irving Berlin's music in a revue called *Watch Your Step* in 1914. Here the show and its audience were talking the same musical language. Fortuitously, now, the threat and finally the reality of war not only brought a heightening of national consciousness but also interrupted the stream of musical imports, especially those of German or Viennese origin. Victor Herbert, Sigmund Romberg (1887–1951), and Rudolf Friml (1879——) went on writing in the operetta vein, but the budding American style was nurtured and increasingly relished.

Whereas Berlin at this time wrote mainly for revues, Jerome Kern (1885–1945) became concerned with the development of an integrated musical play. He had been writing for assorted revues, with some success, when he began collaborating with Guy Bolton in a series of musical comedies that consciously sought to avoid the clichés and conventions of the trade. Their aim, as Bolton put it, was "straight, consistent comedy with the addition of music," free of irrelevant slapstick and interpolated chorus lines.

The shows, produced in the small Princess Theater between 1915 and 1917, were *Nobody Home, Very Good Eddie, Have a Heart*, and *Oh, Boy* (with P. G. Wodehouse joining the team in the last two). Their acceptance seemed to confirm Bolton's

Bridge to the Present

conviction that the American public liked realism, and that the musical comedy had matured to the point where it could depend "as much on plot and character development for success as on music." The first fruits of that viewpoint really emerged a decade later in Kern's *Show Boat*. With that work, the musical comedy came of age. In many ways, *Show Boat* (for which Oscar Hammerstein II wrote the text, based on Edna Ferber's novel) set the course for the development of the American musical for the next three decades. It drew its plot from American literature; it engaged an adult theme; and it integrated music and characterization, song and play with a realism that distinguished it from operetta, in a popular idiom that distinguished it from opera.

When *Show Boat* was produced in December of 1927, the musical comedy had already attained considerable maturity, and Kern's talent and skill were no isolated phenomenon. George Gershwin and Irving Berlin were producing for an avid public; *A Connecticut Yankee* had just created for Richard Rodgers (1902———) a place beside them; Cole Porter (1892–1964) was beginning to be noticed; Hammerstein, Lorenz Hart (who wrote Rodgers's lyrics) and Ira Gershwin had disclosed special writing gifts; and skill in stagecraft had been demonstrated in productions ranging from Ziegfeld Follies spectacle to Princess Theater intimacy. At this moment Broadway was blessed with talent commensurate with its booming prosperity. But this was, for the musical theater as for so much else, a fateful time.

Three months before *Show Boat* appeared, the film *The Jazz Singer* was released, and Al Jolson soon was heard singing "My Mammy" from the screens of movie palaces all over the country. The sound film, coupled with the collapse of prosperity, altered the whole field of entertainment. If *Show Boat* pointed a direction in which the musical play might develop, the coming of the film musical and then the Depression assured that road would be taken. Their public diminished by the new medium, and their financial resources pinched, musical producers sought an audience that looked to the theater for pleasures of the mind as well as the senses. For that audience, creative talent and sophisticated wit were more reliable attractions than gaudy production and high-kicking girls. Revues were trimmed from Ziegfeld proportions to those of the tight-knit, fast-moving *Little Shows* of the early 1930's (the *Grand Street Follies* and *Garrick Gaieties* were precedents in the previous decade). Composers like Berlin, Rodgers, Arthur Schwartz (1900——) could now set the writers' sophisticated jibes to music as sharply pointed, current, and vernacular as the words. For the new revue, as Brooks Atkinson wrote of Schwartz's *The Band Wagon* (1931), "you need not check your brains with your hat."

Not only the revue, in which satire had always figured strongly, but also the musical play began to include pertinent social comment. When *Strike Up the Band* came to the stage in 1930, the reviewer in the *New York World* commented, "I don't remember ever before in a musical comedy having noticed or understood what it was all about. Here all is not only clear but startling. Of all things in the world, here is a bitter, rather good, satirical attack on war, genuine propaganda at times, sung and danced on Broadway, to standing room only." George S. Kaufman and Morrie Ryskind, who wrote the play, had their points sharply underlined by George Gershwin's music (and Ira Gershwin's lyrics). The team collaborated immediately in a second political satire, still more tightly integrating action and music, *Of Thee I Sing*. A broad but telling lampoon of American elections and the presidency (with the 1932 election a year in the offing), the piece received the Pulitzer Prize for drama—the first time the award had been given to a musical play.

Bridge to the Present

Satire was not to be the only or even the principal vein of musical comedy in the decades to follow. But a medium capable of both the drama of *Show Boat* and the barbed wit of *Of Thee I Sing* clearly was not narrowly limited in its possibilities. As the 1930's began, the musical comedy had in hand a fluent American musical vernacular to match its popular form and language, and a remarkable number of talented men creating in its terms. Its most productive years were still ahead.

AMERICAN COMPOSERS: A NEW GENERATION

If the dividing line between "popular" and "classical" was becoming less relevant for the American listening public, it was becoming more critical for the American composer whose creative goals followed the tradition of European musical art. The public loved dance music and the songs of Tin Pan Alley and had learned to enjoy Beethoven, Wagner, Schubert, Liszt, and Dvorak. The American composer was neither content to produce the one nor capable of being the other. Nor did the Gershwin example, when it came, suggest a course open to more than a very few. Among the company of Tin Pan Alley, Gershwin's diversion into concert music roused wonder, but little desire (and less hope) to follow suit. Trained in Germany or by German-trained teachers, the mature American composer had no working familiarity with the idiom of American popular music and furthermore wished none.

In the second decade of the century, Arthur Farwell saw the young composer in America being "lured into" the tragedy of being "trained to make a product that will not be wanted."

The composer, on whose education primarily *as a composer* much money has been spent, finds himself in a perplexing situation; he discovers that his country will accept and pay readily enough for his services as teacher, performer, etc., but that it apparently has no use for him *as a composer*, the very thing he has been educated to be. What he has to give, his country does not want; and it does not tell him what it does want. . . . In fact, there is no connection at all, in a serious way, between the American composer and his country.

When Farwell published these lines, in 1912, Charles Ives (1874–1954) at his creative peak had ceased to concern himself with the connection. He had early resigned himself to composing in his free time, for his private satisfaction, while pursuing (successfully) a career in life insurance. Ives had tried to find understanding listeners for his music in the first years of the century, but what he was writing was so unconventional that the few musicians who saw or heard it responded almost invariably with puzzlement, anger, or scorn. Asked why he did not write music people might like, he could only reply helplessly, "I can't do it—I hear something else!" To have something played, it seemed to him, you had to "write something you do not want to have played." He refused.

In Europe at this time, the first rumblings of a new musical order were being heard in Arnold Schoenberg's *Pierrot Lunaire* (1912) and Igor Stravinsky's *Le Sacre du Printemps* (1913), works which brought before a largely resistant public some of the same musical departures Ives was experimenting with in obscurity and isolation. In 1912, fifteen-year-old Henry Cowell (1897–1965) astonished the San Francisco Music Club with compositions in which he played the piano not only with his fingers but with his whole forearm, creating "tone-clusters" of white or black keys. Cowell's influence, like that of Schoenberg and Stravinsky and Ives, would be felt later among his generation of American composers. For the moment, conductors who dutifully included American music in their programs were likely to select something by one of the reliable traditionalists of the

Bridge to the Present

Boston school—George W. Chadwick himself, or one of his pupils: Horatio Parker, Henry Hadley (1871–1937), Frederick S. Converse (1871–1940). Converse's opera *The Pipe of Desire* was produced at the Metropolitan in 1910, the first opera by an American accorded that distinction; and Parker's *Mona* arrived on the same stage only two years later.

So it was, for the moment. But the moment was over with the war. The war proved to be a powerful catalyst that hastened changes already underway. The efforts of Americanists like Farwell and the Wa-Wan composers were bent away from Europe. New influences were suggesting possibilities beyond European tradition, beyond the traditional altogether. Such were the Armory Show of Cubist and Futurist paintings in New York in 1913, the visit of Diaghilev's Ballet Russe (from Paris) in 1916, and the concerts of the Russian Symphony Orchestra, which Modest Altschuler founded in New York in 1903, and which toured widely during the next two decades.

With the war, the restrictive hold of the German tradition on American concert music was broken. The flow of young musicians to Germany for study ended abruptly. In 1921 Leo Sowerby (1895–1968) went to Rome as the first composing fellow of the American Academy; in the same year, Aaron Copland (1900———) discovered in the new American school of arts at Fontainebleau a brilliant teacher named Nadia Boulanger, who was to help train a dozen or more of the leading American composers of the next decades.

Unlike those of the earlier generation, who had often gone to Europe to study organ, piano, singing, many of the young American musicians now going abroad were bent on careers in composition. Paine, Buck, Chadwick, Foote, MacDowell, Gilbert had won for the serious American composer a respected if

157

limited place in the country's concert life. The work of that generation also meant that musicians who arrived in Europe in the decade after the war were composers already beginning to master their craft, not adolescents seeking their first professional guidance. Paine had gone abroad to study at nineteen, Mac-Dowell at fifteen. But Walter Piston (1894———) was thirty and a Harvard graduate when he came to Nadia Boulanger's studio. Howard Hanson (1896———) had already graduated from a Nebraska college, studied at the Institute of Musical Art in New York and at Northwestern University, and was head of the fine arts department of a college in California when he went to Rome as a fellow of the American Academy in 1922. Roy Harris (1898———) Virgil Thomson (1896———) and Douglas Moore (1892———) were all in their mid-twenties when they went to Paris; and Roger Sessions (1896———) had studied at Harvard, Yale, and the new Cleveland Institute of Music and had begun teaching before he went to Europe as a Guggenheim fellow.

For the new generation, the European experience meant contact not with nineteenth-century musical tradition but with twentieth-century musical ferment. With old values fading, an American's ideas were as welcome as anyone's in marking out what the new values were going to be. Instead of being contemned as lacking any musical tradition, the American was envied his supposed freedom from its baggage, especially if he demonstrated a native's familiarity with the new musical language of jazz. In Paris, the group dubbed "The Six" led a heady rebellion against all established forms and argued for "une musique de tous les jours"—an everyday music that looked to jazz and the music hall for its style. These six young French composers (Honegger, Milhaud, Poulenc, Auric, Durey, Tailleferre) were of the same generation as the Americans then ar-

Bridge to the Present

riving in Paris. In their company, the Americans could feel that they had something to give as well as something to gain. Europe now offered more than schooling. It was a circle of colleagues and kindred spirits.

Returning home, the young composer in the postwar years benefited from the groundwork laid by an earlier generation, but he also faced new problems. The earlier generation had returned from studies in Germany to a country whose music was dominated by German classical tradition and German standards. After the war, the tradition and the standards still held for the American musical public, while the young composers returned from Paris and Rome inspired by fresh and revolutionary ideas. Where the earlier generation largely had followed accepted models, the new one sought new forms and its own voice. The returning composer faced a struggle, but he had company, and advantages the older generation had lacked.

The work of the nineteenth-century musical missionaries had begun to bear fruit. Public school music programs, with their ubiquitous bands and orchestras, were leading to an increasing demand for musical training at a higher level. State universities were establishing music departments which in the coming years would, besides their educational function, offer many of America's composers the security of a teaching position along with the assurance of competent performers and a ready audience for their works. And in the 1920's three important endowments created institutions for professional musical training at a higher level than had ever been available in the United States: the Eastman School of Music at the University of Rochester, the Juilliard School in New York (which soon absorbed the Institute of Musical Art), and the Curtis Institute in Philadelphia. Many of the leading faculty members of these institutions were Europeans,

American Music

but Americans were given a chance to teach as well as to study. In time, the difference between European-trained and American-trained musicians was rendered negligible. When Sousa formed his first band in 1892, forty of its fifty members came from abroad; in 1927, all but one of Sousa's eighty-four musicians were American born.

Ernest Bloch (1880–1959), who arrived in the United States in 1916, was the first of a series of important European composers to teach Americans on their own soil. It is hard to know whether he or Nadia Boulanger taught the greater number of major American composers. Roger Sessions, Douglas Moore, Bernard Rogers (1893———), Quincy Porter (1897–1966), Randall Thompson (1899———) all came to Bloch in Cleveland in the 1920's.

Young composers venturing on the American musical scene after World War I thus found themselves in remarkably good company. But if they wanted an audience, they would have to build it. There was a new kind of missionary work to be done, and several set about doing it. The mission was to make the public aware that musical art had not exhausted itself with Brahms and Wagner, that it was living and growing in the present. It was to engage the interest and encouragement of listeners in behalf of those who were creating new music. A public that had been taught to think of "appreciation" of established "masterworks" had to be taught to think of experiment and adventure.

The first step was to get the new music performed. With that aim Edgard Varèse (1885–1965) and Carlos Salzedo (1885–1961), both French expatriates living in New York, organized the International Composers Guild. Manifestos were the order of the day in art, and the Guild issued one upon entering the

Bridge to the Present

scene in 1921. "The composer," it said, "is the only one of the creators of today who is denied direct contact with the public."

It is true that in response to public demand, our official organizations occasionally place on their programs a new work surrounded by established names. But such a work is carefully chosen from the most timid and anaemic of contemporary production, leaving absolutely unheard the composers who represent the true spirit of our times. . . . The present day composers refuse to die. They have realized the necessity of banding together and fighting for the right of each individual to secure a fair and free presentation of his work.

The Guild was only the first of a series of efforts dedicated to the same goal. The second grew directly out of it. The League of Composers was formed in 1923 by a group that split off from the Guild and commenced giving concerts of its own. Refusing either to restrict itself to "first American performances" as the Guild was doing, or to concentrate on music as genuinely avant-garde as the Guild's, the League sought primarily to provide a platform for American composers. A major contribution of the League was the publication of the quarterly journal, *Modern Music*, begun in 1924. For twenty-three years—until "modern music" no longer had to struggle for recognition—it provided an international forum for broad and penetrating discussion of current musical production and thought, most of it written by composers themselves.

Many of the composers emerging at this time were still anxious (as Aaron Copland said of himself) to discover a style of writing that would be immediately recognizable as American. At the same time, they increasingly felt themselves part of a "modern music" movement that embraced their European counterparts. Both the International Composers Guild and the League of Composers saw to it that major works by such men as Arnold Schoenberg, Igor Stravinsky, Anton Webern, and Paul Hindemith were performed in the United States along with those of Americans. After the International Society for Contemporary Music was founded in Europe in 1922, an American section was not long in forming. And though Varèse disbanded his Guild in 1927, saying its mission had been accomplished, he soon launched a Pan American Association of Composers to give concerts of new music by composers of all the Americas in cities of the Western Hemisphere and, later, in Europe.

Composers returning from European ventures applied themselves to the task of gaining a hearing for their own works and their colleagues'. Aaron Copland, home from Paris, allied himself with the League of Composers, and then joined with Roger Sessions to arrange the series of Copland-Sessions concerts of new music given in New York between 1928 and 1931. Howard Hanson, back from Rome to take over the direction of the new Eastman School in 1925, quickly inaugurated an American Composers Project at Rochester. When this "effort to discover and perform new works that had not yet received performances" was announced, Hanson's office was quickly flooded with manuscripts. The number of annual concerts soon rose from one to five, and an American Music Festival was added. In its first ten years, the project (including the Festival) saw the performance of more than two hundred works, most of them for the first time.

Henry Cowell, who had been too absorbed in his experiments in California to go abroad, launched a project of his own. He founded a New Music Society, began giving concerts in San Francisco in 1926, and the following year began publishing the scores of "ultra modern works" in the format of a quarterly magazine called *New Music*. The first issue was devoted to a

Bridge to the Present

work for chamber orchestra, *Men and Mountains*, composed in 1924 by Carl Ruggles (1876———), a New Englander who liked to write his strongly individualistic music on sheets of wrapping paper, marking the notes in heavy crayon on a staff hand-ruled with lines an inch or so apart. The work had been performed in a concert of the International Composer's Guild, but printed in *New Music* it caught the eye of Charles Ives, who promptly ordered twenty-five subscriptions to the magazine! Cowell, who had heard of Ives, now became curious about his music. He called on the fifty-four-year-old composer-insurance man in his New York office, looked at some of his scores, and persuaded Ives to let him publish something. They agreed on the second movement of the *Fourth Symphony*, which Eugene Goossens actually had performed at Town Hall, New York, in 1927.

It was the first of a number of Ives's works issued by *New Music*, and the beginning of a devoted effort on the part of Cowell and his associates to gain recognition for a composer whose significance only a few were beginning to sense. Another twenty years would have to pass, however, before Ives's music would come into its own. Besides Ives and Ruggles, *New Music* introduced in print such composers as Wallingford Riegger (1885–1961), Ruth Crawford (1901–1953), the orientalist Colin McPhee (1901–1964), and later John Cage (1912———) and Henry Brant (1913———), whose experiments were strongly affected by those of Varèse, Ives, and Cowell.

Support from other sources was also forthcoming for the composers' efforts to secure a place for themselves and their music. When Joseph Pulitzer died in 1911, he left a million-dollar endowment to establish the New York Philharmonic as a permanent orchestra, and another bequest to provide annual traveling scholarships (the first in 1917) for promising composers who might gain from a stay in Europe. The Guggenheim Foundation began awarding yearly fellowships to composers in 1925. Mrs. Elizabeth Sprague Coolidge had opened her estate in the Berkshire Hills for concerts of new chamber music as early as 1918. In 1925, the concerts were moved to the Library of Congress in Washington. There the Coolidge Foundation provided not only a new auditorium in which substantial festivals of chamber music could be held every few years but also funds to pay performers, to commission new works, and to award prizes to noteworthy new music. Prizes for new works were fast multiplying. The National Federation of Music Clubs had been conducting contests for American composers since 1907 and the Society for the Publication of American Music had been selecting scores for its award since 1919. Once electrical recordings had brought the leading American orchestras onto disks and a measure of prosperity to the record companies, the Columbia Phonograph Company and RCA Victor both offered prizes for symphonic works by Americans. The radio networks would provide commissions for composers in the next decade.

As the 1920's gave way to the 1930's, American composers were winning through. The major orchestras were now performing the works of a new generation, and in conductors such as Serge Koussevitzky, Fritz Reiner, Frederick Stock, and Leopold Stokowski the new music had found real champions. Anxiety over the emergence of "an American music" had waned as it became increasingly clear that there were to be several American musics, ranging from the bold abstractions of Varèse to the neo-Romanticism of Hanson, from the classicism of Piston and the atonality of Sessions to the city rhythms of Copland and the prairie spaciousness of Harris. It had been a struggle, and the struggle was not without losses. Charles T. Griffes (1884–1920)

Bridge to the Present

died a decade before he could enjoy the recognition and the opportunities that would certainly have opened to him. And Charles Ives proved a full generation ahead of his time. Before recognition came, he had stopped composing. But in the music he composed and finally saw accepted, he triumphantly conjoined very nearly the whole range of the musics America had struggled to bring forth. A younger generation found in his music resources of individualism, spontaneity, and freedom from convention that lent impulse to fresh musical expression and experimentation.

VIII

Many Musics, Many Audiences

The American composer's particular problem was only beginning to be grasped when it was submerged momentarily in the more general problem of the Depression. The economic emergency combined with the effects of radio and sound films to put tens of thousands of performing musicians out of work. To preserve their skills and avoid their having to undertake "manual assignments for which they were unfitted," the government established a Federal Music Project under the Works Progress Administration. The program, initiated in 1935, soon employed some ten thousand musicians in work that ranged from playing in symphony orchestras or dance bands to teaching music to classes of rural children and collecting and transcribing folksongs.

More than 150,000 public performances were given under the project, in schools, hospitals, and other tax-supported institutions, with a total audience of some one hundred million. Though

Many Musics, Many Audiences

the primary aims of the project were to put musicians to work and to broaden the base of the musical audience, it also served American composers, by including their music in countless programs. By 1938 the project had brought performances of well over five thousand works by some fifteen hundred American (or American-resident) composers. Through Composers Forum-Laboratory programs, in which new works were tried out and discussed, the project tried further to bridge the gap between venturesome composer and puzzled listener. Forum-laboratories, begun in New York in 1935, soon were set up in cities across the country.

When the Federal Music Project was discontinued in 1941, not only had it helped to tide musicians over an economic emergency, but it also had taken concert music to people who had never heard a live symphony or string quartet. And it had broken significant ground in cooperation between national and local, public and private organizations. Each of the project's programs required the material support of sponsors in the local community, and these included universities, city and county governments, chambers of commerce, school boards, musicians union locals, chapters of the National Federation of Music Clubs, and other civic groups.

The base of support for the country's symphony orchestras continued to broaden. At the same time, it became plain that they could never become self-sustaining while fulfilling the educational and cultural role that gave them a place in their communities. Annual deficits were made up by contributions of thousands of individuals (nearly five thousand in the case of the Boston Symphony in 1963) in more than a thousand communities. The orchestras, ranging from twenty-five "major" ones to the orchestral equivalents of community "little theater" groups, were a distinguishing feature of mid-century American musical life.

Baltimore in 1916 set the precedent of appropriating municipal funds to supplement the individual contributions that sustained the city's symphony orchestra. Other cities followed it the years between the wars, often making their contributions in the form of payment for services—concerts to be played for school children, or "municipal concerts" with little or no charge for admission.

Further support was forthcoming from business corporations and charitable foundations. Foundations in the 1960's were contributing more than thirty million dollars annually to cultural institutions. In a growing number of cities and states, arts councils were formed to coordinate the complex web of financial support from individuals, corporations, foundations, and from municipal, state and even federal government which sustained local cultural institutions, including musical ones. Coordinated art centers were planned, incorporating concert and opera stages, after the pattern of the Lincoln Center for Performing Arts in New York, or the projected John F. Kennedy Center for Performing Arts in Washington, D. C. The establishment of a National Foundation on the Arts and Humanities by the Eighty-ninth Congress was a step toward federal assistance to musical institutions firmly rooted in the local communities.

From the 1920's on, colleges and universities assumed increasing importance in providing and stimulating musical activity, until at mid-century campuses in every part of the country were centers of a highly decentralized musical culture. At first geared mainly to preparing future music teachers and supervisors for public schools, the music departments of large state universities

Many Musics, Many Audiences

developed into virtual conservatories-on-the-campus, offering professional training for composers and performers.

Leading creative musicians were invited to become "composers in residence," and for the sufficiently accomplished young composer, joining a university or college musical faculty was the surest means of securing a livelihood. And not only a livelihood. The university's resources of performers, both faculty members and students, provided a ready laboratory for his work, and the campus guaranteed an interested and intelligent audience.

More than a few of the music schools had a "string quartet in residence," often a recognized concert ensemble whose members gave individual and ensemble instruction in their university. University symphony orchestras often reached a level of proficiency that would allow a composer to write for them as he might for a professional ensemble. And in the numerous university "opera workshops" that developed after World War II, it appeared that the opera had finally become domesticated to the United States.

The workshops' aim was to give student musicians an opportunity for practical experience on the stage or in the pit in works of many periods and styles. Directors of remarkable ingenuity and professional competence managed the whole gamut, including operas by a growing number of composers newly attracted by the possibilities of workshop performances. A composer's chances of having a new opera performed by the major companies in New York, Chicago, or San Francisco were small enough to discourage almost anyone from setting himself, uninvited, the task of composing a work with their huge apparatus in mind. By the mid-1950's the existence of more than a hundred opera workshops, on campuses or in local communities in thirty-four states, offered the composer a field worth exploring.

American Music

The opera workshop movement received sharp impetus from the striking success in 1947 of two operas by Gian-Carlo Menotti (1911———), *The Medium* and *The Telephone*. The first had been written on a commission from the Alice M. Ditson Fund for production by Columbia University's opera workshop during the university's 1946 contemporary music festival. It made so strong an impression that a group of producers decided to take it to Broadway, with a professional cast and *The Telephone* as a curtain raiser. The double bill's success was unprecedented for a straight operatic work in the Broadway theater; Menotti's writing clearly was not in the vein of musical comedy or operetta.

Menotti's success did not set any trends on Broadway. To a number of American composers, however, it suggested fresh possibilities of writing for the musical stage: for small cast, small orchestra, small theater, setting the English language in the angular recitative of contemporary musical style, relieved by the lyricism of song-like arias. Only a few aimed at Broadway or any professional stage as they wrote such operas. Indeed, Menotti's own operas, such as *The Consul* (1950) and *The Saint of Bleecker Street* (1959), were the only such works that approached acceptance on Broadway. They had in mind instead the opera workshops, which welcomed new pieces that could broaden a student's musical horizon while offering a possibly opera-shy audience a work of musical theater, in English, in the operatic rather than the Broadway tradition.

Broadway had, indeed, developed a musical theater of its own, in a vein that consistently revealed new musical and theatrical capacities. The synthesis suggested by *Show Boat* and *Of Thee I Sing* was deepened and sharpened by the collaboration of Richard Rodgers with the writer Lorenz Hart in *On Your Toes* (1936) and *Pal Joey* (1940). The latter was based on mordant

Many Musics, Many Audiences

and sophisticated stories by John O'Hara. *On Your Toes* ventured to amalgamate ballet into the musical, with a sequence choreographed by George Balanchine carrying forward the plot. The increasing importance of the dance in the musical, not as mere ornament or diversion, but as an integral part of the dramatic line, was notable in productions like Rodgers's *Oklahoma!* (1943) and Frederick Loewe's *Brigadoon* (1947) (both with choreography by Agnes de Mille), and in Leonard Bernstein's (1912———) *West Side Story* (1957). In the latter, Jerome Robbins's choreography extended beyond isolated dance sequences to share equally in a total music-drama-dance expression.

The synthesis of play and music, in popular vernacular terms, was developed to such a fine art in works like Cole Porter's *Kiss Me Kate* (1948), Rodgers's *South Pacific* (1949) and operetta-like *The King and I* (1951), Frank Loesser's *The Most Happy Fella* (1956), and Loewe's *My Fair Lady* (1956) that the line between Broadway musical and opera became difficult to define. Only the failure of certain works to win public acceptance seemed to suggest when the line had been crossed. Such was apparently the case with *Street Scene* (1947) by Kurt Weill (1900–1950) and with Bernstein's *Candide* (1956), both of which would await revival in the opera house. Weill, who immigrated to the United States in 1939, had his Broadway successes—most notably *Lady in the Dark* (1941) and *Lost in the Stars* (1949). His thorough skill as a composer and orchestrator set standards for other composers in the field, and the influence of his style was strong on younger composers like Bernstein and Marc Blitzstein (1905–1964). It was Blitzstein who adapted Weill's *Die Dreigroschenoper* of 1928 as *The Threepenny Opera*, which enjoyed long and repeated runs in many cities after it was presented in New York in 1954. Weill's folksong opera, *Down in the*

Valley (1948), became a favorite vehicle of the university and amateur opera groups for whom he intended it.

If the line between the vernacular musical theater and opera was becoming blurred, so was that between jazz and traditional music. Jazz itself had significantly changed and developed in the hands of the musicians who played it in the scant decades since it had emerged from New Orleans. Just before the Depression, the early New Orleans style of playing had given way to music arranged for larger dance bands. While not all such bands played music genuinely stemming from jazz, some, like the bands of Fletcher Henderson, Duke Ellington, Bennie Moten (later led by William "Count" Basie), had learned how to preserve jazz flavor and spirit while playing within the framework of a dance-band arrangement. With the end of Prohibition and as the Depression began to ease slightly, the kind of music they played, now dubbed "Swing," swept the country in 1935 as a teen-agers' fad. The "king" was the clarinetist Benny Goodman (1909——) whose band was broadcast across the country every Saturday night from whatever bandstand it happened to occupy at the time in its triumphant travels from coast to coast.

One of the heirs of Chicago jazz, Goodman took his band of the mid-thirties through sharply disciplined but vivid performances of arrangements written by Henderson and often inspired by Basie. As had been the case with New Orleans jazz, "swing" again found white musicians achieving commercial success with music of Negro invention. Negro bands had their successes, however. And it was in the "swing era" that the color line began to break down in jazz groups. Goodman determinedly set the precedent in the mid-1930's by bringing the Negro pianist Teddy Wilson into his band for an engagement in a Chicago hotel.

Many Musics, Many Audiences

"Swing" meant, among other things, big bands (thirteen or more players), virtuoso performers and technically brilliant arrangers. If this was jazz, then jazz had little more to do with the spontaneous improvisation of unschooled folk musicians. Indeed, by the 1940's, jazz musicians whether Negro or white were often conservatory-trained and immensely skilled as instrumentalists or in the arranger's new and special art of composing and scoring. The art lay in writing music for jazz players that either actually left room for improvisation or flowed with so much freedom of invention that it *sounded* as if the players were improvising as they read the notes.

That art (which Ellington and Basie already knew) was obscured as "swing" declined in a frenzy of overscored music for oversized bands ("progressive jazz" was the catchword). It was rediscovered, and the spirit of jazz with it, in a deliberately rebellious-sounding music called "bop" (or "bebop" or "re-bop"), which began to be heard in New York toward the end of World War II. Its protagonists, the trumpeter "Dizzy" Gillespie and, above all, the saxophonist Charlie Parker reacted against the size, weight, and impersonal quality of the swing band; working again with smaller groups, they emphasized solo improvisation in which they explored harmonic and melodic territory strange to jazz, but part of a new, personal, often eccentric musical expression. Those who heard them came to listen, not to dance.

"Bop" had appreciably stretched the jazz vocabulary when it merged almost imperceptibly, in the late 1940's, into something that came to be called "cool" jazz. Parker was an idol of "cool's" adherents, and in many ways it was a continuation of "bop." But instead of the sometimes torrential, explosive outbursts that characterized "bop," "cool" jazz musicians like the trumpet-players

173

American Music

Miles Davis and Chet Baker, the pianist Lennie Tristano, the saxophonist Gerry Mulligan, and the arranger Jimmie Giuffre preferred a relaxed, flowing line. In their music, solos often enjoyed congenial contrapuntal company and the melody on which the group was improvising might be heard, understated but still there.

In all this process of change, the art of writing for jazz performance was becoming progressively refined and sophisticated, as was the art of the performance itself. By mid-century, the various trends were amalgamated in "modern jazz," which was nothing more nor less than a form of chamber music written for jazz-trained musicians, often incorporating improvisation and seeking to preserve the "blues" feeling that was the soul of jazz.

What was there, then, to differentiate this kind of chamber music from the kind traditionally heard in concert halls? Indeed, jazz was no longer a stranger to those halls. Ever since the Goodman band had played a "swing concert" in Carnegie Hall in 1938, but especially after the war, jazz groups found attentive audiences in concert halls around the country. The subtle improvisations of the Modern Jazz Quartet, when the group appeared in the 1950's, were clearly intended to be heard under concert conditions (or on the phonograph), not to the accompaniment of cabaret noises. Furthermore, the musical thought of many of the modern jazz musicians was strongly affected by their acquaintance with the music and techniques of composers from Bach to Schoenberg. Some now recognized the possibility of creating a music out of the convergence of jazz and traditional music. It would not be, like *Rhapsody in Blue*, traditional concert music with jazz flavoring; nor would it be, like some modern jazz improvisation, jazz performance with classical allusions. It would be a new music drawing freely on the technical and formal resources of both traditions. One of its leading exponents, Gunther Schuller (1925———) coined a cognomen for it: "Third Stream Music."

Though a tendency toward merging of forms was observable in some of America's music at mid-century, it was not dominant in the country's musical life. Rather, musical activity was marked above all by its variety—by the number of separate, clearly different kinds of music being made.

The popular music industry underwent far-reaching changes under the impact of radio, phonograph and sound films. "Tin Pan Alley"—the old publishing houses in New York's 28th Street, where songwriters had ground out ballads to be plugged in dime stores and sold in sheet music form to perhaps a million parlor piano-players—ceased to exist. As early as 1919, the Victor company had discovered that a song hit could be made through recordings, without its ever being published in sheet music form. As the rush of musical films began in the 1930's, the film companies drew most of the available songwriting talent to Hollywood, and then bought up the publishing houses to capitalize on the demand for copies of the movies' new songs. The number of new songs multiplied at an enormous rate, and their life-span, with a few exceptions, dwindled accordingly. In the early 1920's, a new song might have been expected to remain popular a year or longer; in the 1950's it was expected to endure for a few weeks and to sell a quarter of a million printed copies, but perhaps a million recordings. The parlor piano gave way to some 22,000,-000 phonographs, 2,000 radio and television "disk jockeys," and 500,000 "juke boxes." In this market, quality was secondary to mass appeal, and the mass most easily appealed to was the teenagers, who indulged their fancy in a succession of musical styles.

Three different but concurrent strains of popular music could be seen running through the period from the 1920's to mid-century: music of predominantly white dance bands, and songs of the Tin Pan Alley stripe; Negro popular music first catalogued by record companies as "Race," later as "Rhythm and Blues"; and "Country and Western" music stemming from rural string bands. As the mid-point of the century passed, elements of Anglo-American and Afro-American popular and folk music were combined at first crudely in "Rock and Roll," then—with a British performing group called the Beatles as catalyst—in countless variants of "Rock."

The volume of the popular music industry was huge, but it represented only one of several vital strains of musical activity. Jazz, in its various manifestations from "New Orleans Revival" to the modern, continued its development quite apart from the mass market. So did the musical comedy. A considerable segment of the public had come to appreciate the peculiar qualities of both these forms, and this constituted a large enough audience that theater composers and jazz musicians were largely freed of the earlier economic necessity to appeal to the mass. They could be confident of a more limited but still sizable public responsive to more sophisticated music.

Activity in the field of folk music, too, had grown steadily since the 1930's. The pioneer work of turn-of-the-century folklorists was given new momentum when the British scholar Cecil Sharp (with Olive Dame Campbell) published, in 1917, a treasury of folksongs he had discovered in the mountains of Tennessee and North Carolina, where they had been handed down from generation to generation since colonial days. Sharp's *English Folk Songs from the Southern Appalachians* had been preceded by John Lomax's collection of *Cowboy Songs and Other Frontier Ballads* (1910), in which such songs

Many Musics, Many Audiences

as "The Cowboy's Lament," "The Dying Cowboy," "Jesse James," and "Home on the Range" were published for the first time. Now there came a steady stream of books of folksongs collected in Kentucky, in New England, in North Carolina, in the Ozarks, among mountain people, miners, cowboys, migrant workers, and gospel singers—sea chanties, lumbering songs, spirituals, railroad songs, singing games, love songs, songs of the range and of the prison.

The first scholarly studies were followed by collections intended for home entertainment, and soon city people were becoming acquainted with a whole body of music that had survived the frontier. They were fascinated to find that they had an ample American heritage of those songs people sing and share without knowing quite where they come from, just how they travel, or how so many people know them.

John Jacob Niles (1892———) began singing formal folksong recitals in the 1930's, performing songs he had gathered from hill folk in his native Kentucky and arranged for self-accompaniment on mountain dulcimers of his own making. The poet Carl Sandburg published *The American Songbag* (1927) and concluded readings of his poetry by singing folksongs, telling his audiences about their origins and strumming his accompaniment on a guitar. When in 1928 the Archive of American Folk Song was established in the Library of Congress, a major step was taken to preserve and perpetuate the music of the country's oral tradition.

John A. Lomax (1867–1948) and his son Alan (1915———) carried their equipment into the field in 1933 to begin the Archive's collection of recordings of songs, ballads, fiddle tunes, harmonica and banjo pieces, and other American folk music, made where the tradition of performance was unbroken. By 1965, the Archive (now called simply Archive of Folk Song) included some sixty thousand examples, and a recording laboratory established under a grant from the Carnegie Corporation had enabled the library to begin reproducing some of the recordings on disks available to the public.

Folk songs reached an ever wider public during the Depression years, as they were taken up by community singing groups and by singers who understood their potential for boosting morale or for voicing social protest. Folk festivals and "hootenannies" multiplied in the decades before and after World War II, country singers swapping songs with singers from the cities who had picked up their versions on collecting trips or simply from books and a growing catalogue of records.

After the war, singing and listening to folk music became a form of sophisticated entertainment (sometimes seasoned with protest) in concert halls and cabarets. It became, too, a new form of family entertainment as the guitar, banjo, and even the dulcimer joined the piano in American living rooms, and a new generation sang and played "Barbara Allen" and "Old Joe Clark," "Sweet Betsy from Pike," and "John Henry." In the 1960's, the guitar actually displaced the piano as the prevalent musical instrument in American homes.

By mid-century folk music had, paradoxically, become popular, and the popularity was reflected in products of the popular music industry. Like jazz, folk music had its commercial as well as its purist phase. Both prospered.

Musicians had taken measures to assure that their economic status rose as musical activity grew in economic importance. In the last decades of the nineteenth century, tentative local musicians' organizations tried, with no great success, to restrict foreign players' inroads into their opportunities to work. By the 1920's, competition from foreign musicians was no longer an

Many Musics, Many Audiences

issue; local unions of the young American Federation of Musicians (which had taken shape in the last few years of the nineteenth century) were strong enough to wage successful strikes that led to improved working arrangements in major symphony orchestras. Exerting pressure by various means, the A. F. M. had similar success in winning benefits for musicians in the popular entertainment field.

In 1948, when longplaying records threatened to displace musicians in radio stations and elsewhere, the union was able to force record manufacturers to establish a Music Performance Trust Fund. Royalties from the sale of phonograph records were deposited in the fund and then used to pay thousands of musicians each year to perform live concerts and public entertainment programs in hundreds of cities.

The American Guild of Musical Artists was founded in 1936 to offer opera and concert performers and chorus and ballet members an organization parallel to the A. F. M.

The American Society of Composers, Authors, and Publishers, which Victor Herbert was instrumental in founding in 1914, was formed to secure to its members a rightful share of profits from the use of their music by hotels, cabarets, restaurants, and (later) radio stations. ASCAP sold performing rights to its members' works, and divided the fees among the membership. As radio burgeoned, and as ASCAP won its way through legal battles over interpretation of the Copyright Law of 1909, the organization became a force to be reckoned with. In 1940, its power prompted radio broadcasters to form a competitive licensing agency, Broadcast Music, Inc.

The audience for concert music and opera continued steadily to widen. In the 1930's, the pianist Olga Samaroff-Stokowski (1882–1948) began in New York a program of courses designed to give musical laymen a deeper enjoyment of the music they heard at home or in concerts, through simple ear training and theoretical study of musical materials and forms.

Soon Mme. Samaroff was teaching graduate students at the Juilliard School to lead similar courses, and her pupils took the program to cities in every part of the country. In the line of Mme. Samaroff's courses (and Walter Damrosch's broadcasts) followed Leonard Bernstein's brilliant mid-century television lecture-demonstrations, in which the New York Philharmonic Symphony was only one of a number of tools the conductor used to bring listeners new insight into music ranging from Beethoven's Fifth Symphony to jazz.

The development in 1948 of the longplaying microgroove phonograph record was a major factor both in broadening the musical audience and in extending the repertoire of music available to it. It was soon discovered that the phonograph record need not be a mass medium, that a number of different audiences with particular musical interests now existed in sufficient size to constitute worthwhile markets for smaller record-producing enterprises. Numerous small companies sprang up, issuing recordings of music hardly known to the public before, from ethnic music of distant cultures to American folksongs, from baroque and medieval musical rarities to experiments of the avant garde.

At the same time, static-free frequency modulation ("FM") broadcasting brought into being new radio stations particularly suited to transmitting musical programs. Introduced in 1940, FM developed vigorously after the war and especially with the advent of longplaying records. By the 1950's there were over four hundred such stations devoting their programs almost entirely to concert music, literature, and art. There were others devoted to "today's top Twenty" in the popular music field.

Many Musics, Many Audiences

Through all these media, a broad general audience was becoming acquainted with music that extended well beyond the famous "three B's." Beethoven and Brahms dominated the concert hall, but audiences heard with some regularity music by representatives of three generations of American composers. Their works accounted for 5 or 6 per cent of the major orchestras' repertoire in a mid-century season, a small share, but still twice as great as it had been twenty years before.

The earliest composers still heard were MacDowell, Chadwick, Foote, Charles Martin Loeffler (1861–1935), and Charles T. Griffes. More often performed were works by the composers who had come to prominence in the 1930's—Copland, Piston, Harris, Thomson, Cowell, and the somewhat more problematic Sessions and Riegger. To these were now added composers of a younger generation, still writing in traditional forms but with distinct individuality: Samuel Barber (1910——), the ubiquitous Bernstein, Elliott Carter (1908——), David Diamond (1915——), Leon Kirchner (1919——), Peter Mennin (1923——), William Schuman (1910——), Harold Shapero (1920——).

Belatedly, the music of Charles Ives took its place in the repertoire. His *Third Symphony*, performed in New York under Lou Harrison's direction some forty years after Ives composed it, was awarded the 1947 Pulitzer Prize. The award signaled the "discovery" of the aging composer who, before his death, was beginning to be recognized in Europe as at home as a seminal figure in contemporary music.

In the opera house Verdi, Puccini and Wagner were the staples the companies relied on for their existence. Special grants occasionally helped the Metropolitan to produce an American work, but none, from Converse's *The Pipe of Desire* of 1910 to Samuel

American Music

Barber's *Antony and Cleopatra* of 1966 managed to remain in the repertoire. The limited audience interested in new operas had to seek performances by opera workshops, or by a few professional companies working on a smaller scale than the Metropolitan. Foremost among these was the New York City Opera, which in 1957, with the help of the Ford Foundation, began a series of spring festivals in which some forty contemporary operas were to be produced over a ten-year period. Opera was seen occasionally also on television, and several new works were written especially for the medium. The first of them was Gian-Carlo Menotti's *Amahl and the Night Visitors*, produced by the NBC-TV Opera Theater in 1951 and so warmly received that a network performance of it became a Christmas tradition.

Both in the concert field and in opera, American performers were prominent, and the quality of the country's instrumentalists—soloists, chamber musicians, orchestra players—was testimony to the standards of training that often began in school bands and orchestras. Unlike the instrumentalists, American singers with operatic ambitions found scant opportunity for careers in their own country. After they had outgrown the opera workshop there were few stages on which they could gain the experience needed before they might dream of a contract with a major company, and even that did not amount to full-time employment. It was a musical anomaly of the postwar years that several hundred American singers, splendidly prepared for an opera stage nonexistent at home, pursued successful careers in European theaters.

As educational opportunities opened, musically gifted Negro Americans were able to gain the training necessary for careers in concert music. The tenor Roland Hayes (1887———) began in the 1920's a distinguished career as concert singer in the United

States and in Europe. In the next decade the bass Paul Robeson (1898———) and the contralto Marian Anderson (1902———) led a growing list of artists whose achievements helped break down remaining racial barriers at home and enhanced respect for American musical culture abroad.

In the decades between the wars, even as the country's rich folksong heritage was being brought to light, American composers' earlier feeling of a necessity to arrive at a national musical style gradually faded. Those years saw the composition of a few major works that were folkloristic or at least consciously "American," by Copland, Harris, and Thomson, for example. But an international contemporary musical style had begun to emerge in the 1920's and as World War II broke out, America became the custodian of it. Arnold Schoenberg, Paul Hindemith, Bela Bartok, and Igor Stravinsky, the composers whose works and theories set the leading musical trends of the second quarter of the century, led a roster of distinguished musicians who emigrated to the United States to continue their work and, most of them, to teach.

If the search for a national style had been to some extent linked to a dream of a national audience, both ceased to concern the younger generation of composers. Their elders' intense effort of the 1930's to win an audience for new music had not really succeeded, but it had been useful. It had stirred among an important minority an awareness of the composer's work and of his needs; and this awareness had led to concrete measures which enabled composers of sufficient determination to gain a hearing and a livelihood. Universities, foundations, individuals, music clubs, composers' organizations, performing groups, and other institutions offered numberless commissions, grants, scholarships, and awards to encourage the writing, performance, and sometimes recording and publishing of new music. The older generation had felt deprived of a wide audience; the younger generation could feel free of the need for any such consideration. In the decentralized musical culture in which they worked, their music was far less likely to be heard in a metropolitan concert hall than in the recital halls of their own university or during a festival devoted to new music, for which they might travel to another campus or to Europe.

Many composers of the new generation continued to express themselves in familiar musical forms, in symphonies, sonatas, variations, in a variety of styles ranging from neoclassic to expressionist.

But some explored new territory. Breaking with the preceding generation as sharply as that generation had broken with its predecessors, the new avant garde investigated relationships between the spontaneous and the predetermined, between live performance and music produced by electronic means, between music and noise. Though their work pointed in the direction of new aural and aesthetic possibilities, it was still in many ways influenced by jazz, by the techniques of Arnold Schoenberg, and especially by concepts embodied in the work of Charles Ives and Edgard Varèse.

While no distinct "schools" were observable, certain motifs were. One was "aleatory"—music in which greater or lesser parts were left undetermined, to be improvised or decided in the course of the performance. At the other extreme was "total serialization"—music in which melody, rhythm, and counterpoint were worked out with mathematical thoroughness. Possibilities of creating "synthetic sound," first advanced in the 1920's, were now explored with electronic devices. After two years of experimentation at Columbia University, an Electronic Music

Many Musics, Many Audiences

Center was formally established there in 1953. In 1959 its facilities, now shared by Princeton, were increased by the acquisition of an RCA Electronic Sound Synthesizer theoretically capable of generating sounds of any conceivable (or not yet conceivable) nature and combining or juxtaposing them in any way at all, at the command of the composer at the controls.

By the late sixties there were electronic music studios in some two hundred schools of music across the country. But composers by no means ceased creating for players and instruments. A number of universities established special groups for the performance of new music, drawing on the remarkable virtuosity of faculty members and students, many of whom were both composers and performers.

From the popular music industry to the electronic laboratory, American music at mid-century was as pluralistic as American society itself. Across a span of two hundred years a distinctive musical culture had developed, and with it musical forms expressive of American civilization. Nothing was more characteristic of it than that it would continue to change.

Important Dates

1640   *The Whole Booke of Psalmes Faithfully Translated into English Metre* (*Bay Psalm Book*) published at Cambridge, Mass.

1698   Ninth edition of *Bay Psalm Book*, containing the first music printed in New England

1714   Organ installed in King's Chapel, Boston

1720   Thomas Symmes, *Reasonableness of Regular Singing*
       Singing school movement was underway

1721   The first American books of musical instruction: Thomas Walter, *The Grounds and Rules of Musick Explained*, and John Tufts, *Introduction to the Singing of Psalm-Tunes*

1731   The *Boston News Letter* carried the earliest known published notice of a public concert in the colonies

1735   Ballad opera, *Flora*, performed at Charles Town

1744   Moravians established a Collegium Musicum for the performance of vocal and chamber music at Bethlehem, Pennsylvania

1750   *The Beggar's Opera* performed in New York

Important Dates

1750's Protestant missions to southern plantations taught hymns to Negro slaves

1752 Lewis Hallam's London Company of Comedians arrived at Yorktown

1759 Francis Hopkinson's "My Days Have Been So Wondrous Free," the earliest known song by a native American

1761 James Lyon, *Urania*, the first collection of psalms and hymns by a native American

1762 St. Cecilia Society founded in Charles Town
Benjamin Franklin's glass harmonica heard in London

1764 Subscription concerts begun by James Bremner and Francis Hopkinson in Philadelphia

1770 William Billings, *The New-England Psalm-Singer*

1775 John Behrent built the first American piano in Philadelphia

1796 Benjamin Carr's *The Archers* performed in New York

ca. 1800 Camp meetings of the Great Revival spread through the Midwest and South

1801 William Little and William Smith, *The Easy Instructor*, explained how to sing hymns from shape notes

1805 Jeremiah Ingalls's *The Christian Harmony* included folk hymns of rural usage

1808 African slave trade outlawed

1810 Gottlieb Graupner organized the Philo-Harmonic Society in Boston

1813 John Davis began presenting French opera in New Orleans

1815 Handel and Haydn Society founded in Boston

1817 Congo Square in New Orleans opened to Sunday Voodoo ritual

1823 Jonas Chickering began producing pianos in Boston

1825 Manuel Garcia company from Italy presented opera in New York

1828 Thomas D. Rice began performing "Jim Crow"

1835 William Walker, *The Southern Harmony*

1838 Lowell Mason named superintendent of public school music in Boston

1842 New York Philharmonic Society founded by Ureli Corelli Hill

1843 Dan Emmett and partners appeared as the Virginia Minstrels

American Music

Ole Bull, Norwegian violinist, was one of a stream of European virtuosi beginning to tour the United States

1845 *Leonora*, opera by William Henry Fry, performed at Philadelphia

1848–54 The Germania Orchestra, among other groups of German musicians, toured the United States

1849 Mendelssohn Quintette Club formed in Boston to perform chamber music

1850 Jenny Lind, Swedish soprano, began a series of American appearances under the management of P. T. Barnum

1851 Stephen Foster wrote "Old Folks at Home" for Christy's Minstrels

1852 *Dwight's Journal of Music* commenced publication in Boston

1853 Louis Moreau Gottschalk performed in New York
Orchestra of Louis Antoine Jullien, French conductor, appeared in New York and performed music by William H. Fry and George F. Bristow

1864 The Theodore Thomas Orchestra began giving regular concerts in New York

1865 Oberlin Conservatory of Music founded

1866 Tony Pastor's "Opera House" presented variety entertainment in New York
The Black Crook produced in New York

1867 New England Conservatory, Chicago Musical College, and Cincinnati Conservatory founded
William F. Allen, Charles P. Ware, and Lucy M. Garrison, *Slave Songs of the United States*

1869 The Theodore Thomas Orchestra began national tours
Patrick S. Gilmore staged the Great National Peace Jubilee in Boston

1872 The Fisk University Singers, in their second year, gained attention in Gilmore's second Jubilee

1873 Cincinnati May Festivals founded under Theodore Thomas's direction
Patrick S. Gilmore accepted leadership of New York's 22d Regiment Band, soon to be nationally known as "Gilmore's Band"

1875 John Knowles Paine appointed professor of music at Harvard

Important Dates

1876 International Centennial Exposition at Philadelphia
Music Teachers National Association founded
1877 Thomas Edison began experimenting with sound recording
1878 New York Symphony Society founded by Leopold Damrosch
Gilbert and Sullivan's *H.M.S. Pinafore* pirated for performances in the United States
1879 Harrigan and Hart's *Mulligan Guard Ball*
1881 Boston Symphony Orchestra founded
1883 Metropolitan Opera opened in New York
Frédéric L. Ritter's history, *Music in America*
1886 Edward MacDowell returned to Boston after a decade in Europe
1887 Emil Berliner invented the flat disc phonograph
1890 Charles Hoyt's *A Trip to Chinatown*
1891 Chicago Symphony Orchestra founded
1892 Frank Damrosch began People's Singing Classes at the Cooper Union in New York
John Philip Sousa formed his concert band
1895 Antonin Dvorak, in an article in *Harper's*, urged American composers to base a national music on indigenous American song
Cincinnati Symphony Orchestra founded
1896 Representatives of local musicians organizations decided to affiliate with the American Federation of Labor, leading to establishment of the American Federation of Musicians
1897 Ben Harney, *The Rag Time Instructor*
"Storyville" district established in New Orleans
1898 Frank Damrosch began Young People's Concerts with the New York Symphony
1899 Scott Joplin's "Maple Leaf Rag"
National Federation of Music Clubs held its first meeting
1900 Philadelphia Orchestra founded
1901 Arthur Farwell founded the Wa-Wan Press
1902 "Ma" Rainey began singing the blues for cabaret audiences
1903 Minneapolis Symphony Orchestra founded
1904 George M. Cohan's *Little Johnny Jones*
1906 The first Victrolas, phonographs with self-contained horns

American Music

1906–10 Oscar Hammerstein's Manhattan Opera Company

1907 St. Louis Symphony Society formed

1909 Copyright law established the exclusive right of copyright owner to public performance of a piece of music for profit, or to its mechanical reproduction

1910 W. C. Handy's "Memphis Blues"
John A. Lomax, *Cowboy Songs and Other Frontier Ballads*

1911 Freddie Keppard's Creole Orchestra toured in vaudeville
San Francisco Symphony Orchestra founded
H. F. B. Gilbert's *Comedy Overture on Negro Themes* performed by the Boston Symphony

1914 American Society of Composers, Authors, and Publishers formed

1915 Tom Brown's Dixieland Jazz Band in Chicago
Musical Quarterly began publication

1917 Original Dixieland Jazz Band played at Reisenweber's restaurant in New York, made first jazz recordings
Storyville district closed in New Orleans
Cecil J. Sharp and Olive Dame Campbell, *English Folk Songs from the Southern Appalachians*

1918 Cleveland Orchestra founded

1919 George Stoddard's song "Mary" became a hit through the sale of recordings rather than sheet music

1920 Dr. Frank Conrad broadcast music over experimental radio station in Pittsburgh; KDKA began regular broadcasting
WWJ-Detroit inaugurated broadcasts of dance music

1921 Edgard Varèse and Carlos Salzedo founded the International Composers' Guild in New York
Eastman School of Music established at Rochester
Harry P. Harrison and Dema Harshbarger formed a partnership to promote "Civic Music Associations"
Leo Sowerby went to Rome as the first composer fellow at the American Academy; Aaron Copland studied with Nadia Boulanger at Fontainebleau

1923 Juilliard School of Music founded

1923–24 League of Composers was founded and began publishing *Modern Music*

1924 Electrical recording process developed

Important Dates

Curtis Institute of Music established in Philadelphia
Paul Whiteman's "Experiment in Modern Music" introduced
George Gershwin's *Rhapsody in Blue*
Louis Armstrong joined Fletcher Henderson's orchestra at
the Roseland Ballroom in New York

1925 Howard Hanson began the American Composers Project at
Eastman

1926 National Broadcasting Company network established
Henry Cowell began publishing *New Music*

1927 *The Jazz Singer* introduced sound movies
Jerome Kern's *Show Boat*
"Duke" Ellington's orchestra played at the Cotton Club in
Harlem
Carl Sandburg, *The American Songbag*
Columbia Broadcasting System established

1928 Walter Damrosch broadcast weekly Music Appreciation
Hour over NBC
Archive of American Folk Song established at the Library
of Congress
Community Concerts Corporation organized by Arthur
Judson

1930 George Gershwin's *Of Thee I Sing*
Weekly concerts of the New York Philharmonic-Symphony
broadcast by CBS
Howard Hanson's "*Romantic Symphony*," written for the
50th anniversary of the Boston Symphony

1931 Metropolitan Opera began broadcast performances over NBC
Edgard Varèse's *Ionisation* for 13 percussion players

1933 Arnold Schoenberg immigrated to the United States

1935 Federal Music Project begun under the Works Progress Administration
Gershwin's *Porgy and Bess*

1938 Benny Goodman Carnegie Hall concert, climax of the
"swing" era
Roy Harris's *Third Symphony* introduced by the Boston
Symphony under Serge Koussevitzky
Aaron Copland's *Billy the Kid* introduced by Ballet Caravan

American Music

Samuel Barber's *Adagio for Strings* performed by the NBC Symphony under Arturo Toscanini

1939   Charles Ives's "Concord" Sonata (1909–15) introduced by John Kirkpatrick

1939–43   Groundwork of "bop" laid by musicians in Harlem jazz clubs

1940   Richard Rodgers's *Pal Joey*

Frequency Modulation (FM) radio broadcasting introduced

1943   Richard Rodgers's *Oklahoma!*

1947   Charles Ives's *Symphony No. 3* (1904) awarded Pulitzer Prize

Gian-Carlo Menotti's *The Medium* and *The Telephone* on Broadway

Magnetic tape recording gained increasing acceptance

1948   Longplaying phonograph records introduced

1949   First recordings of "cool" jazz

1951   Gian-Carlo Menotti wrote *Amahl and the Night Visitors* for NBC Television

John Cage's *Music of Changes*, composed by methods involving chance

1953   Electronic Music Center established at Columbia University

Rockefeller Foundation granted $400,000 to the Louisville Symphony Orchestra to commission new works over a four-year period

1957   Ford Foundation grant to the New York City Opera enabled staging of annual festivals of contemporary opera

Leonard Bernstein's *West Side Story*

1962   Lincoln Center for the Performing Arts opened in New York

1965   National Foundation on the Arts and Humanities established by the 89th Congress

Suggested Reading

Detailed studies of many aspects of American musical life and history remain to be written. Recently, such books as Henry Kmen, *Music in New Orleans: The Formative Years, 1791–1841* (1966), Julian Mates, *The American Musical Stage before 1800* (1961), and Hans Nathan, *Dan Emmett and the Rise of Early Negro Minstrelsy* (1962) have helped fill the gaps. Only through further scholarship of the sort that underlies these (and the earlier pioneer investigations of Oscar G. Sonneck), focusing intensively on American music species by species, period by period, region by region, will we finally be able to piece together an accurate picture of its practice as it was.

There are, nonetheless, a number of works which will add depth and detail to the narrative sketched in the foregoing pages. I shall mention those I have found most useful.

GENERAL

John Tasker Howard's *Our American Music* (1931, 4th ed. 1965) remains indispensable. Though Howard is concerned principally with music as an art, he touches on popular music and musical theater; he takes note, too, of the development of American musical institutions, from singing schools to ASCAP. Above all, he manages to identify virtually every American composer and song-writer who made any recognizable mark and to fit all into a loose chronological narrative. *A Short History of Music in America* (1957, new ed. 1967), in which Howard collaborated with George Kent Bellows, is half the length and conveys a more general picture of musical activity and institutions.

More readable, and closer to the pluralistic spirit of the subject, is Gilbert Chase, *America's Music, from the Pilgrims to the Present* (1955, 2d rev. ed. 1966). In identifying trends of development and in characterizing both musical content and context, Chase is livelier, less conventional. Still, one finds oneself returning to Howard for his encyclopedic detail. Both Howard's volumes and Chase's include useful bibliographies, and *A Short History* adds a long list of recorded works by American composers.

Wilfred Mellers, *Music in a New Found Land* (1965), is an interesting complement to Howard and Chase. An Englishman, Mellers seeks to get at the character of America's music, and he is especially engaged by the interplay of art and popular forms in our music. His is a work of historical scholarship, but still more of criticism and interpretation. The discography, prepared in England by Kenneth Dommett, is expertly selected to illustrate Mellers's text.

Howard and Chase have included what is valuable and accurate from such earlier works as Frédéric Louis Ritter's *Music in America* (1883) and W. S. B. Mathews's *A Hundred Years of Music in America* (1889). These may still be consulted out of curiosity, and especially for information about the period that was the recent past when they were written. Worth a closer look is a volume titled "Music in America" prepared by Arthur Farwell for inclusion (it is Vol. 4) in a 14-volume encyclopedia, Daniel Gregory Mason, ed., *The Art of Music* (1915). Farwell's characteristic introduction still makes interesting reading, and the historical chapters that follow (mostly by W. Dermot Darby) stand up surprisingly well.

A completely different approach, and a useful one, is that of Quaintance Eaton, ed., *Musical U.S.A.* (1949). Each of its thirteen articles treats the musical history of a particular city or region, enabling a reader to compare patterns of development in, for instance, the Pacific Northwest, Minneapolis, Cincinnati, Baltimore.

The American music best documented historically is jazz, at least

Suggested Reading

from the time of its emergence in New Orleans and especially from the time it was first recorded. Still, writing about jazz in general has tended to be more in a vein of folklore than of history or musicology, to concern itself more with legendary heroes than with recording facts or describing musical means and styles. Gunther Schuller, *Early Jazz: Its Roots and Musical Development* (1968) is an important departure from the practice. Extending into the thirties, it is the first in a projected two-volume study which promises to become the standard work in the field.

Lacking Schuller during the preparation of the present volume, I relied heavily—and without regret—on Marshall Stearns' slim but perceptive *The Story of Jazz* (1956), which remains the best brief but comprehensive account of this music's evolution. An extensive bibliography is included. Among earlier works on the subject, still useful are *Jazzmen* (1939) by Frederick Ramsey and Charles Edward Smith, and Winthrop Sargeant, *Jazz: Hot and Hybrid* (1938, revised 1946)—the former for its impression of the early jazz milieu, the latter for its intelligent treatment of jazz as music. See also Wilder Hobson, *American Jazz Music* (1939).

Hear Me Talkin' to Ya (1955, reprinted 1966), edited by Nat Shapiro and Nat Hentoff, is an anthology of telling quotations from jazz musicians about their music and its environment, from the early New Orleans days to the beginnings of bop. Samuel Charters and Leonard Kunstadt, *Jazz: A History of the New York Scene* (1962), focuses faithfully on its chosen locale from the times of brass bands and excursion boats through the Original Dixieland Jazz Band, Paul Whiteman and Duke Ellington, to Thelonius Monk and Dizzy Gillespie. Leonard Feather, ed., *The Encyclopedia of Jazz* (1960), with its supplement, *Encyclopedia of Jazz in the Sixties* (1966), is a comprehensive "who's who," past and present, embellished with topical articles (for example, an interesting one on "Jazz and Classical Music" by Gunther Schuller). A number of more specialized books on jazz are listed in later sections of these notes.

Cecil Smith, *Musical Comedy in America* (1950), has been for some years the most comprehensive and reliable book on the subject. Because of its wealth of detail it will not be replaced by Lehman Engel's *The American Musical Theater: A Consideration* (1967). Engel's study, however, is unique in approaching the subject analytically from a musical standpoint (as well as historically, as a branch of theater); further, by an artful combination of verbal and visual elements, the volume succeeds in conveying the flavor and spirit of forgotten times on the musical stage.

Sigmund Spaeth, *A History of Popular Music in America* (1948) and David Ewen, *Panorama of American Popular Music* (1957), tell "the stories" of the songs and songwriters in popular favor from colonial times to the present. Julius Mattfeld, *Variety Music Cavalcade 1620–1961* (1962), on the other hand, foregoing narrative and anecdote, simply lists the songs (and some instrumental pieces) Americans were singing and listening to, year by year, as they were published; each year's detailed list is followed by a summary of the year's significant happenings in the cultural, political and social life of the country; and the whole—meticulously researched—makes a fascinating if superficial mosaic of popular music and its times.

Useful in studying almost every aspect of American music is Oscar Thompson, ed., *The International Cyclopedia of Music and Musicians* (1938, 9th ed. 1964). Out of date though it was, the bibliography, dropped from the ninth edition, is still good reason to consult the eighth (1958).

In writing my survey, I naturally had frequent occasion to consult general and specialized works outside the field of music. I shall not attempt to list them, but should mention here two volumes in this series which proved especially helpful: Winthrop S. Hudson, *American Protestantism* (1961), and Maldwyn Allen Jones, *American Immigration* (1960).

NEW BEGINNINGS

We have no clear picture of the place of music in the lives of the first English settlers in North America, for their everyday musical practice went virtually undocumented. Carl Bridenbaugh, in *Vexed and Troubled Englishmen 1590–1642* (1968), notes the place of music in England's culture then and assumes that the Englishmen who emigrated transplanted as much of that culture as they could or would to the New World. The question remains, how much they could or would. Neither Bridenbaugh's *Cities in the Wilderness* (1938) nor the several works of Thomas J. Wertenbaker on colonial Virginia offer more than suggestive tidbits toward an answer.

Early music in New England is better documented, but one-sidedly: from the standpoint of Puritan psalmody. The Puritans

Suggested Reading

recorded their controversies over psalm-singing with zeal; of the secular practice of music in the seventeenth century they left us only a few hints. Percy A. Scholes, *The Puritans and Music in England and New England* (1934) is the standard work on the subject, written to show that the Puritans were not the anti-musical folk earlier histories painted them. Gilbert Chase includes the most interesting and pertinent materials from the literature of the controversies and from contemporary journals (like Samuel Sewall's) which offer clues to other aspects of New Englanders' musical practice. George Hood, *A History of Music in New England* (1846) has further detail on the controversies. *Music and Musicians in Early America* (1964), a collection of articles by Irving Lowens, includes a sensible survey of this earliest period along with careful studies of the *Bay Psalm Book* and John Tufts's *Introduction to the Singing of Psalm-Tunes.* Henry W. Foote, *Three Centuries of American Hymnody* (1940, new ed. 1968) devotes nearly half its text to this period.

The appearance of newspapers in the colonies in the second third of the eighteenth century lightened later historians' work. Largely from this source, Oscar G. Sonneck pieced together his ground-breaking *Early Concert Life in America, 1731–1800* (1907) and *Early Opera in America* (1915), putting all later scholars in his debt. Julian Mates, *The American Musical Stage Before 1800* (1961) brings some of this material into focus by taking Benjamin Carr and *The Archers* as the point of departure for a description of contemporary musical and theatrical practice.

Chase offers the best general account of the musical pastimes and enthusiasms of the eighteenth century "gentlemen amateurs" (including the founding fathers) and also of the emigrant professionals who came to prominence toward the end of the century. In addition to the account in *Our American Music,* John Tasker Howard wrote informative monographs on *The Music of George Washington's Time* (1931) and (with Eleanor Bowen) *Music Associated with the Period of the Formation of the Constitution and the Inauguration of George Washington* (1937). Music is shown in the general context of eighteenth-century colonial city life in Frederick P. Bowes, *The Culture of Early Charleston* (1942), based largely on a study of early issues of the *South Carolina Gazette.*

Catherine Cleveland, *The Great Revival in the West, 1797–1805* (1916), conveys an idea of life west of the Appalachians at this period. Against this background she describes the social and religious phenomenon of the camp meetings, with hymn-singing a significant part of it. The spiritual songs themselves—the transition from psalmody to folk-hymns, the late manifestations of the singing school, the shape-note songbooks—are the special province of George Pullen Jackson. His *Spiritual Folksongs of Early America* (1937, reprinted 1964), *White Spirituals in the Southern Uplands, the Story of the Fasola Folk* (1933, reprinted 1965), and *White and Negro Spirituals* (1944) remain classic studies and collections.

Chase surveys the most significant shape-note songbooks in a chapter on "Fasola Folk," and a prime example of the genre can be seen in a reproduction of the 1854 edition of William Walker's *The Southern Harmony*, published in 1939 by the WPA Federal Writer's Project of Kentucky. A priceless description of "Old Time White Camp Meeting Spirituals" by Samuel E. Asbury is found in the Texas Folklore Society Publications of 1932.

In Chase and in Marshall Stearns, *The Story of Jazz*, can be found in the clearest accounts of Negro music in North America before the Civil War, and particularly of the origins of the spirituals. Charles L. Jones, *Religious Instruction of the Negroes* (1842) tells of slaves' early encounters with Protestant hymnody. Harold Courlander, *Negro Folk Music, USA* (1963) studies the relation of American Negro music to its African roots, and points to African survivals in Negro musical practice in America. Still rewarding is William F. Allen's preface to *Slave Songs of the United States* (1867, reprinted 1929), which retains its sense of discovery. A 1965 edition of this first published collection of American Negro songs is revised for home singing with accompaniments arranged by Irving Schlein; it includes Allen's important preface but omits the original authors' annotations to the individual songs.

Of the many collections now available, I shall mention only three others of special interest: Henry E. Krehbiel, *Afro-American Folk Songs* (1914, reprinted 1962), a pioneer attempt to understand the origins and structure of this music; James Weldon Johnson and J. Rosamond Johnson, *Books of American Negro Spirituals* (1940), the most comprehensive collection of the religious songs; and Lydia Parrish, *Slave Songs of the Georgia Sea Islands* (1942, reprinted 1965), almost as much for its graphic design as for its music.

Hans Nathan, *Dan Emmett and the Rise of Early Negro Min-*

Suggested Reading

strelsy (1962), is more than a biography of Emmett, it is the definitive study of the origins and music of the minstrel show, with significant implications for the history of ragtime and jazz. For the entire period under discussion a uniquely valuable volume is W. Thomas Marrocco and Harold Gleason, *Music in America, An Anthology from the Landing of the Pilgrims to the Close of the Civil War, 1620–1865* (1964). With brief but informative commentary, the authors introduce printed music of some of the period's most characteristic and interesting pieces.

I have not really dealt in my essay with two aspects of early American music which are of historical interest but which lay off the course of the country's musical development: Music of the Moravians and other German pietist sects in Pennsylvania; and that of the American Indians. Chase (1955 ed.) and Howard discuss both and provide some bibliography on them.

BUILDING AND SEARCHING

Though music scarcely figures in it, the six-chapter panorama of the United States in 1800 that begins Henry Adams's *History of the United States of America during the Administrations of Jefferson and Madison* (1891) provides a setting against which the musical development of the period can be better understood. A number of the articles in Quaintance Eaton, *Musical U.S.A.*, are rewarding in connection with the period of musical expansion—for example, those on Minneapolis, the Pacific Northwest, San Francisco. Howard Swan, *Music in the Southwest 1825–1950* (1952) describes music in mid-century mining camps. A. B. Hulbert's composite "diary," *Forty-Niners; the Chronicle of the California Trail* (1931) suggests the place of music, from minstrel tunes to hymns, in daily life on the long way west.

Of several accounts written by traveling performers of this period, *Recollections of an Old Musician* (1899) by the Mendelssohn Quintette Club's Thomas Ryan is especially rich. Ryan does more than recall his experiences on the road; he also writes of the mid-century tours of visiting orchestras (particularly the Germania), of the virtuosi (especially Ole Bull), of Lowell Mason and of Patrick S. Gilmore's Jubilees. Louis Moreau Gottschalk devoted the major part of his *Notes of a Pianist* (1881) to his sojourn in the United States between 1862 and 1865. A 1964 edition with percep-

American Music

tive prelude, postlude and notes by Jeanne Behrend is a study both of Gottschalk and of the period. Exploits of a number of virtuosi are recounted in Arthur Loesser, *Men, Women and Pianos* (1954), a social history of the piano devoted in part to its American development.

The lives of Stephen Foster and Dan Emmett are treated at some length by both Chase and Howard. The latter wrote a biography, *Stephen Foster, America's Troubador* (1934, new ed. 1954); Hans Nathan's book on Emmett has already been mentioned. George Stuyvesant Jackson, *Early Songs of Uncle Sam* (1933) is an account of some of the popular songsters published between 1825 and 1850. Unfortunately, it contains only texts, no music.

Lowell Mason's educational work in Boston, and the many currents to which it gave rise, are discussed in Edward Bailey Birge, *History of Public School Music in the United States* (1928, rev. ed. 1939). Birge's survey is more broadly useful, too, as it traces the development of musical instruction from singing schools to conservatories, the rise of school bands and orchestras, and the growth of educators' organizations.

John Sullivan Dwight, Brook-Farmer, Editor and Music Critic (1898), a friend's tribute by George Willis Cooke, is a sound account of Dwight's life and work. Irving Lowens, writing of "Music and American Transcendentalism (1835–50)" in *Music and Musicians in Early America*, discusses Dwight's pre-*Journal* writings, along with those of his associates in *The Harbinger*, published at Brook Farm. (Lowens appends a list of all writings on music in the Transcendentalist periodicals.) *Dwight's Journal of Music* (1852–81) is an invaluable chronicle of musical activity in the third quarter of the century.

John H. Mueller, *The American Symphony Orchestra: A Social History of Musical Taste* (1951), surveys the growth of the major orchestras from their beginnings. Charles E. Russell, *The American Orchestra and Theodore Thomas*, won the Pulitzer Prize when it was published in 1927. It remains a stirring as well as an informative account, based on two reliable but colorless sources: *Memoirs of Theodore Thomas* (1911), by the conductor's widow, and *Theodore Thomas, A Musical Biography* (1905), edited by George Upton from an autobiographical sketch Thomas had written the summer before he died. Upton's biography is in two volumes, the second of

Suggested Reading

which is a valuable catalogue of Thomas's programs from the Mason-Thomas concerts on.

Henry A. Kmen, *Music in New Orleans, the Formative Years, 1791–1841* (1966) includes an account of the earliest venture in resident opera in the United States. Irving Kolodin, *The Metropolitan Opera 1883–1966* (1966), extends a detailed history of the New York company first published in 1936. John Frederick Cone records the story of *Oscar Hammerstein's Manhattan Opera Company* (1966) in its brief but brilliant appearance in the first decade of this century.

H. W. Schwartz, *Bands of America* (1957), is about military bands, amateur and professional, with a chapter on Louis Antoine Jullien by way of introduction to Patrick Sarsfield Gilmore, who Schwartz considers set off the "band craze" of the 1880's and '90's.

William Treat Upton has written biographies of *Anthony Philip Heinrich* (1939) and *William Henry Fry* (1954), and music by both composers is included in the Marrocco-Gleason anthology, *Music in America*, mentioned earlier. Of the later generation of American composers of the nineteenth century, the *Dictionary of American Biography* includes few, among them, MacDowell, Paine, and Buck; the bibliography of Howard's *Our American Music* includes an index to articles about many other composers.

Antonin Dvorak's call to American composers to recognize their national musical heritage appeared in *Harper's*, February, 1895, under the title "Music in America." Arthur Farwell's reply, in the form of the Wa-Wan Press, is described in an article by Edward N. Waters in Gustave Reese, ed., *Birthday Offering to Carl Engel* (1943).

Ragtime is treated as a distinct genre, apart from jazz, in *They All Played Ragtime* (1950, reprinted 1959) by Rudi Blesh and Harriet Janis; Scott Joplin, Tom Turpin, and John Stark are central figures in the story. Samuel B. Charters, *The Bluesmen* (1967), probes the relation between African music and American Negro hollers, work songs and blues, but the origins of the blues remain obscure.

Stearns summarizes clearly the social and historical currents that led to the amalgamation, in New Orleans, of the music we call jazz. A more extended and still lively account is Samuel B. Charters, *Jazz: New Orleans 1885–1963* (1963); it is a remarkable collection of information on individual musicians which, cumulatively, yields a

American Music

picture of early (as well as later) New Orleans jazz life. Alan Lomax, *Mister Jelly Roll* (1950) describes Creole life in turn-of-the-century New Orleans and also Storyville, as remembered by "Jelly Roll" Morton.

The chapter on minstrel shows in Constance Rourke, *American Humor* (1931) is unrelated to music but rich in insight into the significance of the entertainment and its passing. Cecil Smith, *Musical Comedy in America* deals in detail with the American musical theater following the Civil War. Contemporary accounts of *The Black Crook, The Mulligan Guard* and *Evangeline* can be found in Barnard W. Hewitt, *Theater USA 1668–1957* (1959). E. J. Kahn Jr., *The Merry Partners* (1955) is about Harrigan and Hart, in helpful detail.

EMERGENCE

From the end of the nineteenth century, a succession of American music critics provided a running chronicle in the daily press and in magazines, following concert and opera activities especially. Compiled in books, the writings of some of the best convey a sense of their musical times in terms of activity and of public and professional reaction to it. I mention as examples Richard Aldrich, *Concert Life in New York 1902–23* (1941); Paul Rosenfeld, *An Hour with American Music* (1929) and *Discoveries of a Music Critic* (1936); Virgil Thomson, *The Musical Scene* (1945), and Irene Downes, ed., *Olin Downes on Music* (1957).

Nicholas Slonimsky, *Music Since 1900* (1949), is a chronology of significant events, many in the United States, focused mainly on avant-garde concert music. Abel Green and Joe Laurie, Jr., *Show Biz, from Vaude to Video* (1951), covers the same period, treating music, particularly popular music, as one element in a breezy year-by-year chronicle edited from the columns of the theatrical newspaper, *Variety*. The maturing of musical comedy in this century is treated in detail in the Smith and Engel volumes cited above. Isaac Goldberg, *Tin Pan Alley* (1930), and David Ewen, *The Life and Death of Tin Pan Alley* (1964), describe the popular music industry before and after the advent of radio and sound motion pictures. Some still more recent trends are suggested in Caroline Silver, *The Pop Makers* (1966) (no less pertinent because the protagonists are British); *The New Sound / Yes!* (1966), edited by Ira Peck for a

Suggested Reading

youthful audience; and Burt Goldblatt and Robert Shelton, *The Country Music Story* (1966).

The spirit of community music that prevailed at the beginning of the century is evident in Lucy and Richard Poate Stebbins, *Frank Damrosch: Let the People Sing* (1945). See, too, Arhur Farwell on "Music for the Fourth of July" in *Suggestions for the Celebration of the Fourth of July by Means of Pageantry* (1912), published by the Russell Sage Foundation, and two books that are an earlier generation's counterparts of the Rockefeller Panel and Twentieth Century Fund reports I shall mention later: Augustus D. Zanzig, *Music in American Life* (1932), sponsored by the National Recreation Association, and Frederick R. Keppel and R. L. Duffus, *The Arts in American Life* (1933), prepared for President Hoover's Research Committee on Social Trends.

Roland Gelatt, *The Fabulous Phonograph* (1955, new ed. 1966), traces the history of the American recording industry, with emphasis on the "classical" field.

Lloyd Morris, *Not So Long Ago* (1949), contains a good informal account of the beginnings of radio broadcasting, with some attention to music.

Dixon Wecter, *The Age of the Great Depression 1929–1941* (1949), is useful background for the transition to the latest period in this survey. It includes a brief account of the Federal Music Project, of which a proper comprehensive chronicle seems never to have been brought together.

Alan Lomax, *Mister Jelly Roll*, traces the spread of jazz (through Morton) in the 1920's and 1930's to Chicago, the Midwest, New York, and California. Among many personal chronicles of jazz life in that period, perhaps the most interesting are Louis Armstrong, *Satchmo* (1954), and Mezz Mezzrow and Bernard Wolfe, *Really the Blues* (1946), accounts of two vastly different characters who have candor in common.

Compact critical considerations of key jazz figures decade by decade are provided in Martin T. Williams, *Jazz Masters of New Orleans* (1967); Richard Hadlock, *Jazz Masters of the Twenties* (1965); Ira Gitler, *Jazz Masters of the Forties* (1966); and Joe Goldberg, *Jazz Masters of the Fifties* (1965). A book on the thirties is forthcoming. Less concerned with personalities and more with trends and styles is John S. Wilson, *Jazz: The Transition Years 1940–*

60 (1966), which contains both bibliography and record list. Andre Hodeir, *Jazz: Its Evolution and Essence* (1956), is a perceptive musical analysis by a French jazz musician and critic particularly interested in the developments in the same period. Neil Leonard, *Jazz and the White Americans* (1962), is a social rather than musical study, dealing with the gradual public acceptance of jazz between the wars.

Later tendencies in jazz were followed in a monthly *Jazz Review* published in 1958 and 1959. One of the editors, Martin Williams, compiled a collection of articles from the journal in *Jazz Panorama* (1962). Finally, I mention A. B. Spellman, *Four Lives in the Bebop Business* (1966), for what it conveys of contemporary jazz life, the social as well as musical concerns of its people.

Since folksong collecting really got under way in the 1930's, the literature on folk music has grown steadily, much of it concerned with social and literary rather than musical aspects of the subject. D. K. Wilgus, *Anglo-American Folksong Scholarship Since 1898* (1959), is an informative commentary, not on the music but on what has been written about it; it includes a discography, and list of printed song collections. Ray M. Lawless, *Folksingers and Folksongs in America* (rev. ed. 1965) is a biographical handbook of performers which includes, too, annotated lists of printed collections and of longplaying records. Bruno Nettl, *An Introduction to the Folk Music in the United States* (1962), does discuss music, including that of immigrant groups and Indians.

Rather than attempt to evaluate the many available folksong collections, I mention just three I have enjoyed and learned from: Carl Sandburg, *The American Songbag* (1927); Olin Downes and Elie Siegmeister, *A Treasury of American Song* (1940); and *Folksong USA* (1947), the last book on which John and Alan Lomax worked together, with adroit piano arrangements by Charles and Ruth Seeger.

Henry Cowell, *American Composers on American Music: A Symposium* (1933, new ed. 1962), remains an interesting depression-years status report by young men who later became some of our most respected composers. Aaron Copland, *Our New Music* (1941), is a longer statement by one of them. Gilbert Chase, *The American Composer Speaks, a Historical Anthology 1770–1965* (1966), extends the discussion in time—back to William Billings, up to Earle Brown.

Suggested Reading

Full biographies of some of the best known composers of this century are available; I mention as especially worthwhile Henry and Sidney Cowell, *Charles Ives and His Music* (1955). Further useful sources of biographical information are John Tasker Howard, *Our Contemporary Composers* (1941), for composers active in the 1920's and 1930's; Claire R. Reis, *Composers in America* (1947); and articles in such periodicals as *Modern Music* (between 1924 and 1948), the *Bulletin* of the American Composers Alliance (suspended in 1965), and *Musical Quarterly* (since 1915).

Wilfred Mellers, *Music in a New Found Land*, is particularly rewarding in its discussion of recent composition. The rationale underlying the work of some of the younger composers is explored by Eric Salzman in a chapter of Richard Kostelantetz, *The New American Arts* (1965). Continuing sources of information about new concert music are the "Current Chronicle" of the *Musical Quarterly*, the quarterly *Perspectives of New Music* published under the auspices of the Fromm Foundation, and *Source*, published by a group of avant-garde composers in Davis, California.

The economic and institutional underpinnings of American musical life in the mid-twentieth century are studied in detail in William J. Baumol and William G. Bowen, *Performing Arts: The Economic Dilemma* (1966), prepared for the Twentieth Century Fund. Policy recommendations are developed in a parallel study, *The Performing Arts: Problems and Prospects* (1965), under the auspices of the Rockefeller Brothers Fund. See also Jacques Barzun, *Music in American Life* (1956), Paul S. Carpenter, *Music, an Art and a Business* (1950), Vineta Colby, ed., *American Culture in the Sixties* (1964), Herbert Graf, *Producing Opera for America* (1961), Alan Rich, *Careers and Opportunities in Music* (1964), and Cecil Smith, *Worlds of Music* (1952).

Recordings

There exists no systematic historical anthology of American music on recordings, nor can one be adequately pieced together from the music that has been recorded through the years by various companies, societies and foundations. Further, manufacturers' catalogues are changeful, even ephemeral. A comprehensive discography for this volume would thus be of little value; the list would be spotty, and the reader would inevitably be frustrated in his search for many of the records. The following notes are offered as an informal guide to pertinent examples, all on longplaying records thought to be available without great difficulty.

A few preliminary remarks about certain of the the labels: Recordings in the Music in America series listed here were issued on a a subscription basis by a Society for the Preservation of America's Musical Heritage, in New York. Though the recordings are no longer current, they may be found in many libraries.

The American Recording Society, established in the 1950's with the support of the Alice M. Ditson Fund, has ceased issuing records, but some of its recordings, reissued under the Desto label, are mentioned below.

Recordings

A Carnegie Corporation grant makes it possible for the Library of Congress occasionally to press field recordings from the Archive of Folk Song on longplaying disks for sale to the public. There are 61 such disks at this writing, some of which are referred to below. They may be purchased only from the Library of Congress directly. Among them, it should be mentioned, nineteen are devoted to music of American Indian tribes, most of it recorded in the field by Frances Densmore and Willard Rhodes. The remaining records cited should be available through commercial channels.

NEW BEGINNINGS

A collection of *Early American Psalmody*, in which the Margaret Dodd Singers sing from the Bay Psalm Book, was issued in both the Music in America and the American Recording Society series. It may be found in some libraries. There are, to my knowledge, no other examples of music from seventeenth century America on records. *Child Ballads Traditional in the United States* (Library of Congress) gives field recordings of American versions of British songs that must have come over with early settlers.

A few of William Billings's tunes and anthems can be found in record anthologies: *The New England Harmony* (Folkways), for example, includes some Billings along with music of Jeremiah Ingalls and other early tune-book composers; two Billings anthems are included in the Library of Congress disk of *Sacred Harp Singing;* another is sung by the Robert Shaw Chorale in a collection, *Easter* (Victor); and a charming round, "When Jesus Wept," can be heard in *Golden Ring* (Folk-Legacy), which also includes three folk hymns. Sixteen folk hymns from early nineteenth-century tune books are sung by the Shaw Chorale in *Sing to the Lord* (Victor).

Francis Hopkinson's *Eight Songs* of 1788 are sung by Thomas Hayward, with harpsichord, in a Cambridge recording. James Hewitt's piano or harpsichord sonata, "The Battle of Trenton," published in 1797, is performed by E. Power Biggs in *The Organ in America* (Columbia). The Moravian Music Foundation has seen to the recording of arias, anthems, and string trios by some of the eighteenth-century *American Moravians* (Columbia), notably John Antes and J. F. Peter. Peter and two obscure musicians active in Philadelphia and New York in the 1790's, Jean Gehot and J. C.

American Music

Moller, are represented in *American Colonial Instrumental Music* (Folkways). While there are no recordings of early American ventures in ballad opera, *The Beggar's Opera* (London) is an example of the British prototype.

Negro Folk Music of Africa and America (Folkways), edited by Harold Courlander, records relationships that may date back to early American history, though we have no way of knowing just what West African music sounded like three hundred years ago, nor how it may have been adapted at that time by those who were brought over as slaves. The Library of Congress's *Afro-American Spirituals, Work Songs, and Ballads* suggests the "wild and unaccountable" something that fascinated early observers of Negro singing in America, as does *Negro Religious Songs and Services* in the same series. *The Fisk Jubilee Singers* (Folkways), spirited as they are, sing their spirituals in concert arrangements several removes from the songs' origins.

BUILDING AND SEARCHING

Piano Music of Louis Moreau Gottschalk is recorded by Eugene List (Vanguard) and Amiram Rigai (Decca). Symphonic music of the period by Bristow, Fry, and Paine was recorded in the Music in America series. Of the later generation, the following examples can be cited:

Horatio Parker: Hora Novissima (1893) (Desto)
Edward MacDowell: *Suite No. 2 for Orchestra* ("Indian") (1897) (Desto, Mercury); *Piano Concerto No. 2 in D Minor* (1890), *"Woodland Sketches" for piano* (1896), *Piano Sonata No. 4* ("Keltic") (1901) (Vanguard)
George Whitefield Chadwick: *Symphonic Sketches* (1902) (Mercury); Symphonic Ballad, *Tam O'Shanter* (1911) (Desto)
Arthur W. Foote: *Suite in E for Strings* (1910) (Mercury)

Though the music of American Negro minstrelsy has not been reconstructed on records, *Minstrel Songs of the Nineteenth Century*, arranged by Hershy Kay and issued in the American Recording Society series, at least revived some of the melodies.

Early ragtime piano can be heard in a number of Riverside recordings transcribed from piano rolls; they are out of print at this writing, but may reappear. All of Scott Joplin's rags are played by

208

Recordings

John "Knocky" Parker in *Original Ragtime Compositions* (Audiophile). Selections from Joplin's opera *Treemonisha* (1911), performed by a Utah State University group, are recorded on the Portents label.

The beginnings of jazz in New Orleans—street bands, rags, blues—are documented in the 11-disk historical anthology, *Jazz* (Folkways). Pre-New Orleans (or extra-New Orleans) factors in the music that became jazz are suggested in the Library of Congress recordings of *Afro-American Blues and Game Songs, Negro Blues and Hollers,* and *Negro Work Songs and Calls,* as well as in the two related Library of Congress disks mentioned earlier. For country blues, some early, some later, see *Country Blues* (Folkways), edited by Samuel Charters; *Really! the Country Blues* (Origin Jazz Library); *Big Bill Broonzy Sings Country Blues* (Folkways).

EMERGENCE

The 11-record Folkways history, *Jazz,* documents compactly the development of jazz from New Orleans early in the century to performances of Dizzy Gillespie and Lennie Tristano in the 1940's. The following are further examples of the various jazz styles represented in the anthology, with some additions illustrating later developments. The list is meant to be suggestive, not comprehensive. The dates are those of the recording sessions.

Original Dixieland Jazz Band (1917–18) (Victor)
King Oliver (1923) (Epic)
Louis Armstrong's Hot Five and *Hot Seven* (1925–28) (Columbia)
The Bessie Smith Story (1925–30) (Columbia)
King of New Orleans Jazz: Jelly Roll Morton and His Red Hot Peppers (1926–28) (Victor) Regrettably no longer available is the Riverside pressing of *The Saga of Mr. Jelly Lord,* taken from Alan Lomax's sessions with Morton at the Library of Congress in 1938.
The Bix Beiderbecke Story (Columbia)
Fletcher Henderson: A Study in Frustration (1923–38) (Columbia)
Duke Ellington: At His Very Best (Victor). *The Ellington Era* (1927–40) (Columbia)
Count Basie and His Orchestra (1938–39) (Decca)
Benny Goodman Carnegie Hall Jazz Concert (1938) (Columbia)

American Music

Billie Holiday: *The Golden Years* (Columbia)
Stan Kenton: *Artistry in Rhythm* (Capitol)
Dizzy Gillespie: *Groovin' High* (Savoy)
Charlie Parker: *Greatest Recording Session* (1945) (Savoy)
Miles Davis: *Birth of the Cool* (1949–50) (Capitol)
Thelonius Monk: *Work!* (1954) (Prestige)
Lennie Tristano (1955) (Atlantic)
Modern Jazz Quartet: *Fontessa* (1956) (Atlantic)
Jimmy Giuffre 3 (Atlantic)
Gerry Mulligan: *Genius* (1960) (Pacific Jazz)
Ornette Coleman: *At the Golden Circle* (1966) (Blue Note)
John Coltrane: *Expression* (1967) (Impulse)

Complete recordings of musical shows are, in part, a sign of the increased integration of form in recent decades. By the same token, such recordings of shows (excluding operettas) antedating *Show Boat* are nonexistent, nor are the George M. Cohan musicals, for example, likely to be revived for recording. Accordingly, the following list begins with excerpts from two characteristic operettas in recordings current at this writing, then proceeds to a selection of representative shows of the last four decades, mostly in "original cast" recordings. The dates are those of the original production, not of the recording.

Victor Herbert: *Naughty Marietta* (1912) (Capitol)
Sigmund Romberg: *The Desert Song* (1926) (Capitol)
Jerome Kern: *Show Boat* (1927) (Columbia)
George Gershwin: *Girl Crazy* (1930) (Columbia)
Harold Rome: *Pins and Needles* (1937) (Columbia)
Richard Rodgers: *Pal Joey* (1940) (Columbia)
Rodgers: *Oklahoma!* (1943) (Decca)
Leonard Bernstein: *On the Town* (1944) (Columbia)
Irving Berlin: *Annie Get Your Gun* (1946) (Decca)
Kurt Weill: *Street Scene* (1947) (Columbia)
Cole Porter: *Kiss Me, Kate* (1948) (Columbia)
Frank Loesser: *Guys and Dolls* (1950) (Decca)
Revue: *New Faces of 1952* (Victor)
Jerome Morross: *The Golden Apple* (1953) (Elektra)
Bernstein: *West Side Story* (1957) (Columbia)

In attempting a useful list of examples in the field of popular music of this century, one boggles at the sheer numbers of record-

Recordings

ings, of types, of representatives of each type. The recordings in the brief list below were chosen for being typical and available.

History of Jazz: The New York Scene 1914–45 (Folkways) principally for James Reese Europe's Society Orchestra of World War I days
Roots: Rhythm and Blues (RBF)
Early Rural String Bands (Victor)
Ballads and Breakdowns of the Golden Era (1926–31) (Columbia)
Paul Whiteman's Orchestra: *Featuring Bing Crosby* (1928–29) (Columbia)
Guy Lombardo: *Sweetest Music This Side of Heaven* (1926–39) (Decca)
Glenn Miller: *The Chesterfield Broadcasts* (1940–42) (Victor)
Frank Sinatra: *The Early Years* (Columbia)
Rock, Rock, Rock (Chess)
Bob Dylan: *Times They Are A-Changin'* (Columbia)
Country Music Festival (Starday)
The Jefferson Airplane: *Crown of Creation* (Victor)

In the list of American folk music recordings that follows, a number of examples stem from earlier periods in the country's history. Only in the last half-century has there developed any wide public awareness of them or interest in their existence, hence the general listing at this point. A broad introduction to the field is provided in *The Ballad Hunter* (Library of Congress), edited and narrated by John A. Lomax; in *Folk Box* (Elektra), and in *An Anthology of Folk Music* (Folkways).

Generally, folk music recordings can be divided into two categories: those made in the field by more or less scientific collectors, the performers being people for whom the music is part of a directly inherited local folk tradition (the Library of Congress recordings are the prime example); and those in which the singers or players are collectors or professional performers who learned the music by studying the performance of musicians in the first category. With a few exceptions, these examples are in the traditional category.

Library of Congress recordings (in addition to those mentioned earlier): *Anglo-American Ballads; Anglo-American Shanties, Lyric Songs, Dance Tunes and Spirituals; Play and Dance Songs*

American Music

*and Tunes; American Sea Songs and Shanties; Railroad Songs
and Ballads*
Negro Folk Music of Alabama (Folkways)
Music Down Home (Folkways)
The Cowboy: His Songs, Ballads, and Brag Talk (Folkways)
Old Time Fiddle Classics (Country)
The Ritchie Family of Kentucky (Folkways)
Traditional Music of Beech Mt. North Carolina (Folk-Legacy)
Carl Sandburg Sings His American Songbag (recorded 1952-53)
   (Caedmon)
Leadbelly's Last Sessions (Folkways)
Woodie Guthrie: *Dust Bowl Ballads* (Victor)
The Weavers at Carnegie Hall (Vanguard)

American composers of the twentieth century are increasingly
well represented in recordings, though music of certain early figures
such as Arthur Farwell and Henry F. B. Gilbert is still missing from
the catalogues. The following list, approximately chronological,
suggests some of the leading trends of the last six decades.

Anthology, *Songs by American Composers* (Desto), including songs
   by MacDowell, Ives, Griffes, Barber, and others
Charles E. Ives: *The Unanswered Question* (1908) (Columbia);
   Pieces for Chamber Orchestra, and Songs (Cambridge); *Sym-
   phony No. 4* (1910) (Columbia); *Piano Sonata No. 2* ("Con-
   cord") (1909-15) (CRI)
Charles T. Griffes: *Roman Sketches* (1917) (Lyrichord); *The
   Pleasure-Dome of Kubla Khan* (1919) (Mercury)
Henry Cowell: *Tone-Cluster Pieces* (1912-30) (CRI)
George Gershwin: *Rhapsody in Blue* (1924) (Columbia, Decca);
   Concerto in F (1925) (Mercury, Columbia); *Ella Fitzgerald
   Sings Gershwin Songs* (Decca); *Porgy and Bess* (1935) (Co-
   lumbia)
Edgard Varèse: *Octandre* (1924), *Integrales* (1925), *Ionisation*
   (1931) (EMS, Columbia); *Poeme Electronique* (1958) (Colum-
   bia)
Carl Ruggles: *Sun Treader* (1933) (Columbia)
Roger Sessions: *Concerto for Violin* (1935) (CRI)
Aaron Copland: *Piano Variations* (1930) (Concert-Disc, Odyssey);

Recordings

Rodeo (1942) (Columbia); *Appalachian Spring* (1944) (Columbia)

Howard Hanson: *"Romantic" Symphony* (1930) (Mercury)

Virgil Thomson: *Four Saints in Three Acts* (1934) (Victor)

Roy Harris: *Third Symphony* (1938) (Desto, Mercury, Columbia)

Walter Piston: *Symphony No. 2* (Desto)

Samuel Barber: *Adagio for Strings* (1936) (CBS and others); *Piano Sonata* (1949) (Victor); *Vanessa* (1958) (Victor)

Wallingford Riegger: *Music for Brass Choir* (1948–49) (CRI); *Symphony No. 4* (1957) (Louisville)

Leonard Bernstein: *Fancy Free* (1944) (Columbia); *Serenade for Solo Violin, Strings and Percussion* (1954) (Columbia)

Gian-Carlo Menotti: *The Medium* (1946) (Columbia)

Leon Kirchner: *String Quartet No. 1* (1949) (Columbia)

Elliott Carter: *String Quartet No. 1* (1951) (Columbia)

Harry Partch: *The Bewitched* (1957) (CRI)

John Cage: *Variations II* (1961) (Columbia)

Earle Brown (b. 1926): *Available Forms I* (1961) (Victor)

Gunther Schuller: *Transformations* (1957), in an anthology, *Outstanding Jazz Compositions of the 20th Century* (Columbia)

Lukas Foss (b. 1922): *Echoi* (1963) (Epic)

Charles Wuorinen (b. 1938): *Piano Variations* (1963), in an anthology, *New Piano Music* (Advance)

Milton Babbitt (b. 1916): *Ensembles for Synthesizer* (1966) (Columbia)

Electronic Music from the University of Illinois (1966) (Heliodor)

Acknowledgments

I am indebted to helpful librarians in the music library at the University of Chicago, the Newberry Library, Chicago, the Amerika Haus (USIS) Library, Hamburg, and the Music Division and Archive of Folk Song of the Library of Congress. David Minter, now of Rice University, made many valuable suggestions on reading an early version of the manuscript.

The book would not have been begun without the stimulation and encouragement I received from Daniel J. Boorstin. It would not have been finished except for the persistent confidence of my dear wife.

Index

Index

Index

Index

Index

Index

Index

Index

Index

Index

Index

Index